The Art of Worship

The Art of Worship
Opening Our Eyes to the Beauty of the Gospel

Paxson H. Jeancake

Wipf and Stock Publishers
Eugene, Oregon • www.wipfandstock.com

THE ART OF WORSHIP
Opening Our Eyes to the Beauty of the Gospel

ISBN: 1-59752-715-7

Cataloging-in-Publication data

Jeancake, Paxson H.
The art of worship : opening our eyes to the beauty of the gospel / Paxson H. Jeancake.

Eugene, Ore.: Wipf and Stock Publishers, 2006

xiv + 172 p.; 23 cm.

ISBN: 1-59752-715-7

Includes bibliographical references.

1. Public worship. 2. Liturgics. I. Title.

BV15 . J34 2006

Manufactured in the U.S.A.

For more information about the author visit:
www.rhythmofworship.com

Or write to:

Rhythm of Worship
P.O. Box 1639
Woodstock, GA 30188

Contents

Foreword

ONE OF the happiest developments in recent evangelical theologies of worship is the emphasis on gospel-centeredness. If the Great Commission is the distinctive task of the church, then the gospel must suffuse all aspects of the church's life and ministry, including worship. In our services, we need to hear and speak much more about how far we have fallen and how great has been God's grace to us in Jesus Christ. Traditions and contemporary practices that hinder the centrality of grace must be rooted out, and we need to do more careful thought on how each element of the service can proclaim the good news.

Paxson Jeancake's book is a great help in that regard. It began as an integrative paper under my supervision for Reformed Theological Seminary, and it really does integrate many areas of theological study: exegesis, church history, systematics, epistemology, practical theology. Jeancake achieves this integration, to some extent, with the help of a scheme of three perspectives that I have expounded in my own writing and teaching. The applications to worship are Paxson's own: the theology of worship, the community of worship, and the leaders of worship. Theology sets forth the biblical norm. Community is the context, the "situational perspective" to which the norm is applied. The focus on leaders is an "existential perspective," a discussion on how God transforms people by his grace to lead the worship of his people.

We can see all of this as a description of how the gospel works on us. It comes as a divine message (norm) into a communal context, to specific people, so that those people, by grace, gain a passion for praising and sharing the love of God for us in Jesus Christ. Through them, in turn, God communicates this love and praise to the people in the congregation, and all lift up their hearts and voices in praise of God's grace.

The existential focus here is on leaders, though, more than on the congregation as a whole. Jeancake's specific interest is to encourage churches to recognize the arts as a legitimate divine vocation, indeed a church vocation. In the process of bringing the gospel to bear upon people, Jeancake argues, art plays a major role. We see that in the biblical tabernacle and temple, in the poetry of the Psalms, the object lessons of the prophets, the parables of

Jesus, the vivid symbolism of apocalyptic. Jeancake fights an uphill battle contending for the arts in a Presbyterian-Reformed environment, with its tradition of artistic minimalism. But he is on solidly biblical ground, and he makes a good case for encouraging the gifts of Christian artists in the ministry of the church.

Besides his broad vision, he helps us here with many of the nuts and bolts of worship, commenting on different orders of worship, assembling and training worship teams, mentoring, dealing with problems. In all of this, he maintains his basic focus on God's grace and shows us how to relate the nuts and bolts to this larger vision.

I am very grateful for this book. My own writing in this area is more narrowly focused. *Worship in Spirit and Truth* (Phillipsburg: P&R, 1996) is largely a normative perspective, setting forth biblical principles. *Contemporary Worship Music* (P&R, 1997) is situational, interacting with the debate at the time over the content of worship, especially music. My colleague Reggie Kidd's recent *With One Voice* (Grand Rapids: Baker, 2005) supplies an existential perspective, asking us to experience worship through the eyes and hearts of different kinds of worshipers. Jeancake's book, however, brings these perspectives all together, giving a bird's eye view of how they relate to one another and interact.

Further, amid all our talk about "gospel-centered" worship, Jeancake shows us what it actually looks like and feels like, and how it can become a practical reality. He expounds well the *richness* of the different elements of worship: the many different types of hymns, creeds, and prayers, the depth of the symbolism of the sacraments, the power of the word in preaching, and how these can be enhanced by the arts. His discussions of hot-button issues in this regard like drama and multi-media are balanced and cogent.

He suggests many ways in which we may vary these elements week to week, in order better to bring out different aspects of their biblical meaning. He quotes and refers to many sources that worship leaders can use in preparing worship, including confessions and creeds, sample orders of worship and prayers drawn from different traditions. He urges us to be aware of the ethnic and cultural contexts of our congregations, including the particular kinds of idols that oppose the gospel in those neighborhoods. He has much to say about making use of the diversity of gifts that God gives to each congregation. I appreciated especially his advice on helping people "navigate through change," including ways of distinguishing between good change and bad change. He introduces readers to a great deal of really helpful literature on worship.

I could say much more, but in doing so I would virtually have to go through the book page by page. Suffice it to say that I'm delighted that this book will now be available to God's people. May God use it to raise up leaders with vocations in the arts, and to enrich the worship of God's people to the glory of Jesus and his gospel.

John M. Frame
Professor of Systematic Theology and Philosophy
Reformed Theological Seminary, Orlando, Florida
Author of *Worship in Spirit and Truth, Contemporary Worship Music,* and
The Doctrine of God

Preface

THERE IS a season in my journey as a worship leader that I don't think I will ever forget. While working and studying as a graduate student, I was leading worship for various ministries in Birmingham, Alabama, including the singles' ministry and worship team at my church. At this point in my life, at the age of 24, I was still trying to figure out my dreams and calling. I had lived in Nashville for a year after graduating from college and thought that maybe a career as a singer/songwriter was my dream. One particular weekend I met a friend in Memphis to rehearse some songs for a potential recording project—songs I had written about life, roads, towns and other topics of a more coffeehouse setting and style. While this dream went by the wayside, God had a greater purpose for that weekend.

Before heading back to Birmingham, my friend reminded me of a worship song we used to sing in college entitled, "His Banner Over Me," written by Kevin Prosch. I brought that song back to Birmingham and began using it in the various worship communities I was leading. My pastor heard me sing it and asked if I could lead it one Sunday morning. This was a big deal because up to that point I was simply strumming away behind the fichus tree on stage, virtually unseen and mostly unheard!

So one Sunday morning, towards the end of the song set, I walked out from behind the fichus tree, stepped up to the mic with my guitar and led the congregation in "His Banner Over Me." That was a crossroads kind of moment for me, personally, and for the life of this relatively young church plant. I believe God began to use that song to open people's eyes to the truth of God's love in a powerful way.

In time and space, God used Solomon to pen the words of Song of Songs 2:4, using the metaphor of a banner; he used Kevin Prosch to turn that metaphor into song; and then he used that song to set that truth on fire in the midst of a congregation in Birmingham, Alabama.

There were times when we would sing that song that you could sense the presence of God in a very powerful way. Leading corporate worship brought me a joy and satisfaction greater than any dream I had of singing about roads and towns in coffeehouses in Nashville.

More recently, my wife, Allison, and I led some seminars on worship for several churches desiring to explore the intersection of gospel, art, and worship. Several months after the seminars, a worship leader friend shared a very powerful story of someone who attended the conference with a plan to take her own life. A woman had come to the worship gathering because she had "paid her five bucks." Through the combination of song and prayer that woman left with a renewed sense of hope, resolved not to take her life. The specific prayer that was a factor in saving this woman's life is from a collection entitled *The Valley of Vision*. A portion of that prayer reads, "Let me learn by paradox that the way down is the way up, that to be low is to be high . . . that the valley is the place of vision."[1]

I had no idea when I was planning that service that a woman would come, hear that prayer, find that "the valley is the place of vision," and walk away radically changed by the powerful dynamics of corporate worship.

Each and every Lord's Day there is the potential for such moments of spiritual illumination and transformation to occur in the lives of God's people. As a worship leader, it is my priestly duty to help retell the gospel story and message. Each week, it is my job to craft, write, select, find, uncover, and borrow: prayers, themes, texts, lyrics, melodies, and images—all for the purpose of helping us experience and express the beautiful, paradoxical truth of the gospel. What an awesome privilege. What a serious responsibility.

This book is meant to serve as a resource for exploring the intersection of gospel, art, and worship. It is meant to offer perspectives on the topic of the artistic media of worship and the way such expressions are fleshed out in the context of community and through the gifts of hungry and thirsty worship leaders. Gospel-centered worship does not happen in a vacuum.

I am indebted to many people as I think about this project.

To my pastors over the years: Rick Holmes, Wesley Horne, Ted Strawbridge, Bob Flayhart, and Scotty Smith. You have served as my gospel heroes, week in and week out. With your words and with your transparent lives you have served as living letters, teaching me more about the gospel than the latest book, buzz word, or seminar.

To Reggie Kidd and Wade Williams. Thank you for teaching me how to love the church—that community is so much sweeter than stardom. Though we are beyond the walls of the classroom, I will also be learning from you.

To Steve Childers. Your passion for the gospel is contagious! Thank you for giving me a forum to create and refine much of the content in this book.

To my close friends and fellow worship leaders on the front lines: Greg Hill, Darrell Trickett, Phil Mershon, Matthew Means, Steven Wooddell, and Jonathan Gilley. I love catching up and playing with you guys. You have helped sustain me on this journey.

To Matt Luchenbill, James Roach, and Brian Retzlaff. Our Tuesday mornings together have shown me that I can bear all and not be condemned.

To the people of East Cobb Presbyterian Church. What a privilege to worship together through all of the various seasons of our church. Thank you for letting me flesh out so many of these thoughts and experiences in the context of real gospel community.

To Ellen Beaver. Thank you for your many hours of editing. You're good!

To the friends in small groups over the years. What amazing community we have enjoyed. May we always be hungry for God's word, intentional about loving one another, and quick to extend an invitation.

To John Frame. I will forever think in triads. I hope you realize the gift you are to the Church.

To Mom, Dad, and Elizabeth. God has written such an interesting story for our lives. Mom, thank you for being the provider in so many ways. Dad, your hand has always been the strongest to hold. Elizabeth, what a wonderful sister you are and have been. How thankful I am for the many things we share in common—a love of music and the arts, a desire to live near the ocean . . . the adventure of raising two little girls!

To my daughters, Laura Camille and Mallory. I'll let you in on a little secret . . . there is nothing you could do that would cause me to love you any more or any less than I do right now.

To my wife, Allison. You are my sweetest voice, most intimate ally, closest friend. You speak truth into my life. You keep me from hiding. You support my dreams. I truly love you.

To the true Worship Leader, the one who sings over us, my Redeemer and Lord. Thank you for hearing the innocent prayer of a young teenager years ago. Thank you for the oceans and the deserts of this journey and for letting me play the guitar once again.

NOTES

1. Arthur Bennett, ed., *The Valley of Vision* (Carlisle, Pa.: Banner of Truth Trust, 1975).

Introduction
Perspectives on Gospel-Centered Worship

Leadership

(Part One)

Life & Community
Ministry Qualifications
Kingdom Investments

Gospel-Centered
Worship

Theology

(Part Two)

Story
Imagery
Expression

Community

(Part Three)

Personal Relationships
Liturgical Models
Cultural Context

Figure 1: Three Perspectives on Gospel-Centered Worship

Organizational Structure:
Leadership, Theology, and Community

As BEGIN our journey we must first acknowledge that gospel-centered worship does not happen in a vacuum. Gospel-centered worship is crafted and facilitated by human leadership, informed by biblical inquiry and theological conclusions, and fleshed out in the context of a local culture and community. The organizational structure for this book is built upon these three categories (leadership, theology, community) and employs the

1

unique "tri-perspectival" (three perspectives) approach developed by John Frame.

In his groundbreaking work, *The Doctrine of the Knowledge of God*, Frame introduces his approach through the technical vocabulary of the "normative," "situational," and "existential" perspectives. Frame's approach allows one to view various subjects from the vantage point of Scripture, the world, and the self, respectively.

I vividly remember a particular lunch conversation with Professor Frame in which I asked him how he developed his three perspectives approach. He shared with me about his graduate study in philosophy, particularly in the area of epistemology (the theory of knowledge). He shared how students and professors will often study and become enamored with the rationalists (who use reason as their primary method of epistemology), the empiricists (who advocate sensory experience in the material world as the way to know something), or the existentialists (who believe that knowledge of "self" is of prime importance). Often, a person will settle into one of these theories of epistemology (rationalism, empiricism, existentialism) at the exclusion of the other two.

What Professor Frame came to realize is that all three are necessary for a balanced view of epistemology. The rationalists' view of *reason*, the empiricists' view of the *material world*, and the existentialists' view of the *self* are all valid "perspectives" for gaining true knowledge of something. Frame writes:

> The knowledge of God's law, the world, and the self are interdependent and ultimately identical. We understand the law by studying its relations to the world and the self—it's "applications"—so that its meaning and its application are ultimately identical. Thus all knowledge is a knowledge of the law. All knowledge is a knowledge of the world, since all our knowledge (of God or the world) comes through created media. And all knowledge is of self, because we know all things by means of our own experience and thoughts. The three kinds of knowledge, then, are identical but "perspectivally" related; they represent the same knowledge, viewed from three different "angles or "perspectives."[1]

Frame argues that this is nothing less than "generic Calvinism." He demonstrates that Calvin, on the first page of the *Institutes*, "speaks of the interdependence of the knowledge of God and the knowledge of self and then, surprisingly to some of us, states that he does not know which comes first!"[2]

This concept is so important because we tend to focus on one or two perspectives when discussing a given topic. Frame's approach helps us form a balanced view of any subject of inquiry. Frame has applied his approach to other disciplines including Lordship and ethics.

In his book, *The Doctrine of God*, Frame describes how the Lord in Scripture reveals himself in three ways: "by a narrative of his acts, by authoritative descriptions of his nature, and by revealing something of his inner life through the Trinitarian persons. These correspond respectively to the Lordship attributes of control, authority, and presence."[3] Applying his three perspectives approach to the field of ethics, Frame recognizes the role and interdependence of Scripture, situations, and persons. He writes:

> The normative perspective studies Scripture as the moral law that applies to situations and persons; without these applications, the law says nothing. The situational perspective studies the world as a field of ethical action . . . in doing so, it accepts the biblical description of the world and the reality of persons in the world. The existential perspective studies the ethical subject—his griefs, his happiness, his capacities for making decisions—but only as interpreted by Scripture and in the context of his situational environment.[4]

Author and Professor Richard Pratt, once a student of Professor Frame, has employed the three perspectives approach to hermeneutics (the study of all that goes into interpreting the Bible). In his book, *He Gave Us Stories*, Pratt offers students and lay people a method of studying the Old Testament Scriptures. His book is organized around three processes of interpretation: preparation, investigation, application. Each chapter walks the reader through various facets of these three perspectives of interpretation. He writes:

> In this book we are going on a dig into the ancient texts of Old Testament narratives. We will make preparations for our work, investigate the Old Testament in its ancient world, and apply our discoveries to modern life. If we overlook any of these steps, our work with Old Testament narratives will be incomplete . . . We will speak of three major facets in the interpretation of Old Testament stories: *preparation*, *investigation*, and *application* . . . These processes are not entirely separate; they depend on each other in countless ways. Yet each one is essential for understanding Old Testament narratives.[5]

One of my goals is to introduce Frame's approach to the subject of worship. As I mentioned earlier, this book is organized around three perspectives. Part One discusses the existential perspective, focusing on the life and ministry of the worship leader—one who is informed by a biblical worldview and who lives in the context of a gospel-centered community. Part Two deals with the normative perspective, exploring a theology of worship that is fleshed out in the context of community and through the leadership of gospel-centered worship leaders. Part Three deals with the situational perspective, discussing the cultural context and local identity of a worship community that is being shaped by the gospel and the unique character of its leadership.

My discussion on leadership is also organized perspectivally exploring the life and community (existential), ministry qualifications (normative), and kingdom investments (situational) of the worship leader. All three of these perspectives are necessary for a balanced discussion of those involved in leading and facilitating the worship of God's people. A worship leader needs to be preaching the gospel to himself everyday—cultivating the heart of the psalmist, and becoming more and more aware of one's own interior life. In addition, worship leaders need a certain palette of qualifications to be as effective as they can be in their calling. They must view themselves (to some degree) as theologians, as artists, and as pastors. Finally, they must have a vision that is greater than both their own professional dreams and even the dreams of their own local church. Worship leaders need to have a kingdom perspective, investing in the lives of younger, emerging leaders; promoting the advancement and development of graduate-level education; and fostering a missional mindset for their own local culture, for North America, and for the world.

My thoughts on a gospel-centered worship theology are organized perspectivally. The story of redemption serves as the normative perspective of God's inspired word, the written record of divine revelation that we read and hear and apply to situations and persons. The sacraments, visual arts, and aesthetics serve as the situational perspective—images and everyday objects in the world, but signs and seals of the covenant (sacraments) as well as personal and corporate expressions (visual arts and aesthetics) that we see and experience and that are informed by God's word. Finally, the songs, prayers, and professions of faith serve as the existential perspective, the lyrical and poetic language of our faith that we express and that have been shaped and inspired by our world and by God's word.

My discussion in Part Three involves the three perspectives approach, exploring personal relationships (existential), liturgical models (normative), and cultural context (situational) as factors that shape the identity of a gospel-centered worship community. Thus, Frame's three perspectives approach is the basis for the organizational and theological structure of this book.

It is important to note that these perspectives represent not merely theological or philosophical language by which to discuss worship; I believe they actually reveal the very character of God himself, and the way he has initiated his relationship with us as worshippers. The three perspectives allow us to see the way God has given us divine revelation about himself, organically inspired, that we might have intimate knowledge of him; how he has entered right into our world, giving us the common stuff of life (bread, wine, water) to gather around in community, enabling us to see and experience the gospel; and how he has given us the gift of music, the intimacy of conversation, and the heritage of truth through which we voice our own inner affections, petitions, and convictions. This is the way God has set it up. Speaking of worship perspectivally is, thus, not so much man's categorical invention, but language we can employ to recognize God's unique initiative.

Preliminary Considerations: Gospel, Art, and Worship

In addition to being familiar with the structure of this book, it will also be important to clearly define some of the key terms that will be frequently employed, namely, "gospel," "art," and "worship." Thus, before we move through the content of this book we need to be on the same page as far as the meaning of these three terms.

The Beauty of the Gospel

We will begin by asking an obvious, but important question: "What is the gospel?" My own experience and observations resonate with that of Dallas Willard who laments that, in America, when it comes to Jesus and the gospel "presumed familiarity has led to unfamiliarity, unfamiliarity has led to contempt, and contempt has led to profound ignorance."[6] My hope is to gain a fresh hearing of the gospel for those *who think they know it* as much as for those who readily confess that they do not understand its message.

For many, the gospel wrongly connotes a message that is meaningful only once for an individual—to bring him or her to salvation. From then on it becomes a message that is to be *shared* to bring others to a point of personal salvation. Though the gospel is, of course, the message that begins our journey in Christ, it is also the message that *sustains* our journey in Christ until either we perish, or the Lord returns. We should preach the gospel to ourselves everyday. We don't come to know Christ through faith and repentance and then grow in Christ by works. On the contrary, we both begin our walk with Christ, and we *continue to grow* in Christ by these two powerful spiritual dynamics (faith and repentance).

The Apostle Paul articulates this dynamic in his letter to the Galatians:

> You foolish Galatians! Who has bewitched you? Before your very eyes Jesus Christ was clearly portrayed as crucified. I would like to learn just one thing from you: Did you receive the Spirit by observing the law, or by believing what you heard? Are you so foolish? After beginning with the Spirit, are you now trying to attain your goal by human effort? Have you suffered so much for nothing—if it really was for nothing? Does God give you his Spirit and work miracles among you because you observe the law, or because you believe what you heard? (Galatians 3:1-5)

Tim Keller, pastor of Redeemer Presbyterian Church in Manhattan, captures our ongoing need of the gospel in this way:

> The gospel is not just the "A-B-C" but the "A-to-Z" of the Christian life. The gospel is not just the way to enter the kingdom, but it is the way to address every problem and is the way to grow at every step . . . In fact, if the gospel is true, the more you see your sin, the more certain you are that you were saved by sheer grace and the more precious and electrifying that grace is to you . . . the gospel gives us enormous power to admit our flaws.[7]

In working with both adults and students I have found that people often have difficulty articulating the gospel in their own words. This is usually a reflection of how presumed familiarity has led to unfamiliarity. It is very easy for the gospel to be lost in the midst of very common, recognizable phrases. Over the years I have found some modern articulations to be very helpful in bringing out the truth of the gospel in a fresh way:

> "You are more sinful than you could ever dare imagine, but you are more loved and accepted than you could ever dare hope." (Tim Keller)

> "Cheer up, you're a lot worse than you think! But God's love and mercy are much greater than you deserve." (Jack Miller)

> "There is nothing you can do to cause God to love you any more; there is nothing you can do to cause God to love you any less than he does right now." (Michael Card)

Yet, even if we maintain a clear understanding and acceptance of the gospel, we still have to preach it to ourselves everyday. In his letter to the Ephesians, the apostle Paul offers the following prayer:

> I keep asking that the God of our Lord Jesus Christ, the glorious Father, may give you the Spirit of wisdom and revelation, so that you may know him better. I pray also that the eyes of your heart may be enlightened in order that you may know the hope to which he has called you, the riches of his glorious inheritance in the saints, and his incomparably great power for us who believe. (Ephesians 1:17-19a)

Though he doesn't use the word directly, in speaking of the Ephesians' "hope," "riches," and "inheritance," Paul is of course speaking of the gospel. The most interesting fact about this passage, however, is that regarding these gospel promises; Paul prays that the eyes of their hearts would be enlightened to them!

The Apostle Paul is not writing to nonbelievers but to *believers* in Christ! What the believers in Ephesus needed above all was a clear knowledge of God, including joyful recognition of God's way for their lives and a willingness to follow his direction. Paul is not saying that we should ask God to give the Holy Spirit to those who have already received him, but rather "that we may and should pray for his ministry of illumination."[8] He is praying that the Ephesians be given "deeper penetration into the meaning of the gospel."[9] According to Stott, Paul's request is that "they may appreciate to the fullest possible extent the implications of the blessing they have already received."[10]

We need our eyes opened to the beauty of the gospel because, like the Ephesians, we often suffer from spiritual blindness and manifest the following symptoms: we don't really understand the gospel, we so easily forget the gospel, we don't really believe the gospel, and we turn to false idols.

Why Do We Need Our Eyes Opened to the Gospel?

We don't really understand the gospel. As we've already discussed, we often live as if the gospel is only for the nonbeliever. We wrongly suppose that as mature Christians we need to get on with the "work" of growing in Christ, thinking that faith and repentance is a one-time event necessary for salvation, not an ongoing dynamic for spiritual renewal.

However, another reason why we don't really understand the gospel is because it is so contrary to our natural way of thinking. In his book, *Not Ashamed of the Gospel*, Morna Hooker writes:

> Our problem is simply that we are too used to the Christian story; it is difficult of us to grasp the absurdity—indeed, the sheer madness—of the gospel about a crucified saviour which was proclaimed by the first Christians in a world where the cross was the most barbaric form of punishment which men could devise.[11]

The cross has become one of the primary symbols of the Christian faith, yet Tidball laments that "long familiarity with it has lessened its absurdity and repugnance and led us to turn it into an item of beauty."[12] In other words, the cross is something we wear around our necks, not something that shapes our lives. The words, "Take up your cross and follow me" have become almost optional for us today. They don't have the same bite that they did to the early Christians. We would rather live lives that are safe and serve a God who is tame.

In his highly significant work, *The Cross of Christ*, John Stott addresses the centrality of the cross as the symbol of the paradoxical, counter-intuitive nature of the gospel. He writes:

> Though crucified in weakness Christ is God's power, and though apparently foolish he is God's wisdom . . . For what men regard as God's foolishness is wiser than their wisdom, and what they regard as God's weakness is stronger than their strength . . . In brief, divine and human values are completely at variance with one another. And the cross, which as a way of salvation seems the height of feebleness and folly, is actually the greatest manifestation of God's wisdom and power.[13]

According to Tidball the message of the cross "exposes our own thoughts and systems as an illusion. It shows our wisdom to be folly, our power to be feeble and our goodness to be inadequate."[14] We need to have our eyes opened to the gospel because it cuts against the grain of worldly wisdom.

We so easily forget the gospel. Even if we maintain a true understanding of the gospel, we so easily forget it as we go about our everyday life. We often live as if the gospel had nothing to say about an anger problem, or about raising children, or about relating to family and friends. An elder at my church recently remarked, quite profoundly, that "All of this talk about the gospel sounds nice until we have to apply it to ourselves!"

Unfortunately, it is often when we need it the most that we tend to remember it the least. We tend to have gospel amnesia when we are faced with the very real issues that stir up guilt and shame. Yet, this is precisely when we need the light of the gospel of Christ to shine most brightly, exposing the darkest corners of our hearts and allowing God's redemptive work to be made manifest through brokenness and humility. Too often we lose sight of the fact that the gospel is able to address every facet of our lives—it is the very insight we need to live as Christians in this world each and every day.

We don't really believe the gospel. Even with a clear understanding and awareness of the gospel, at a deep level, often we simply don't believe it. Ironically, we think it's too good to be true. I truly believe that one of our greatest struggles as Christians is believing that God loves us as much as he says he does. I know, at times, I doubt God's goodness. We need to bathe ourselves in the message of God's word so that we are continually reorienting ourselves to the amazing, unconditional love of God.

In his book *Objects of His Affection* Scotty Smith writes:

> This book is a study and story of the heart's journey in coming alive to the compelling love of God. The chapters that follow wrestle with many of the difficulties and delights of knowing "this love that surpasses knowledge" (Ephesians 3:19).[15]

We all need help in "coming alive to the compelling love of God." We need to have pictures of God in our mind like that of Zephaniah 3:17. Here we see that God delights over us, even sings over us! Reflecting on this passage Scotty writes:

> The first time I read Zephaniah's words about God's delight, I assumed that the prophet must be talking about the great heroes of the faith—believers like Abraham, Moses, King David, Esther, Deborah—the faithful ones who accomplished enough to make God smile . . . But the truth is, Zephaniah is not writing to the noble but to the nincompoops. Those who deserve the judgment of God have become the recipients of his delight. He doesn't just tolerate forgiven sinners. We who have trusted Christ fill his heart with gladness. He hasn't just made room for us in heaven; he has made room for us in his joyful heart.[16]

Many of us need to be reminded of the fact that the gospel is true, that God really does love us as much as he says he does. I vividly remember one of my pastors once vehemently asking our congregation, "Why do you think it's called the *good news?*"

We turn to false idols. Finally, we need our eyes opened to the gospel because we have so many false idols in our lives. We don't worship golden calves and Asherah poles, but the more modern and sophisticated idols of success, safety, comfort, control, and autonomy. These idols are more subtle, and we often bow down to them without even realizing it. In fact, in following after the "American Dream," many of these idols are actually encouraged in our North American culture.

With this orientation to the message of the gospel and the ongoing need to have our eyes opened to it, a final question remains: "*How* does God open our eyes to the gospel?" I will offer four ways that God opens our eyes to the gospel: through the inspiration of his word, through the illumination of the Holy Spirit, in the context of community, and through the power of artistic media.

How Does God Open Our Eyes to the Gospel?

Through the inspiration of his word.

> All Scripture is God-breathed and is useful for teaching, rebuking, correcting and training in righteousness, so that the man of God may be thoroughly equipped for every good work. (2 Timothy 3:16-17)

Here, Paul is sharing with the young Timothy the power of God's inspired word. Scripture helps open our eyes to the gospel, particularly in its "correcting" ability—the word helps correct our false beliefs, our doubts, and our idols.

Through the illumination of the Holy Spirit.

> I keep asking that the God of our Lord Jesus Christ, the glorious Father, may give you the Spirit of wisdom and revelation, so that you may know him better. (Ephesians 1:17)

As part of a powerful prayer to the believers at Ephesus, Paul demonstrates the role that the Holy Spirit plays in illuminating our hearts and minds that we might have a more intimate knowledge of God, that we might know him better.

In the context of community.

> They devoted themselves to the apostles' teaching and to the fellowship, to the breaking of bread and to prayer. (Acts 2:42)

> And let us consider how we may spur one another on toward love
> and good deeds. Let us not give up meeting together, as some are in
> the habit of doing, but let us encourage one another—and all the
> more as you see the Day approaching. (Hebrews 10:24, 25)

Through this picture of the early Church we see the importance of Christian
community in the life of the believer. The writer of Hebrews also encourages us to meet together that we might "spur one another on." God opens
our eyes to his gospel, not only through his word and the Holy Spirit, but
also in the context of Christian fellowship and community.

Through the power of artistic media. In addition to the above means of
grace, God also uses the power of the arts to open our eyes to the beauty
of the gospel. Gregory Wolfe, publisher and editor of *Image: A Journal of
the Arts and Religion*, offers the following definition and function of art:

> At its best, art transfigures the world around us for a brief time,
> strives to the let the radiance of truth, goodness, and beauty flash
> out for an instant. Art wakes us up, trains our perceptions, and re-
> minds us that when we try to build rigid structures around presence
> we inevitably lose what we attempt to keep. The purpose of art is
> not to strand us in an alternate world, but to return us to the realm
> of the ordinary, only with new eyes.[17]

Art has an effect on its recipient. According to Wolfe, it gives us "new
eyes." Thus, art communicates. Speaking to the way in which art communicates, one author writes, "It touches deeper, 'secret chords of feeling,'
realities greater than appearances."[18]

In the next several pages we will look more thoroughly at the role of
artistic media and how God uses artistic means to open our eyes to the
gospel. We will begin by exploring the unique language of art, itself. Then
we will take a biblical survey of the Old and New Testaments, exploring the
use of artistic media. We will begin by exploring the prescriptions for the
temple; then we will reflect on the story of Nathan and David, the ministry
of the Prophets, and finally, the life of Jesus.

The Role of Artistic Media

THE UNIQUE LANGUAGE OF ART

When I was in college I would travel miles with some of my friends to see
David Wilcox in concert. As an artist Wilcox can weave together stories
and songs in such a way that the audience is left mesmerized. During his

concerts "time" becomes something that seems to stand still—something measured not in minutes or seconds, but simply by the essence and beauty of the experience itself. At its best art takes us to places that transcend chronological time and reveals things that are beyond mere description. In these moments the world is a place less about "doing" and more about "being."

I recently heard Tim O'Brien, a musician and songwriter, comment that "art allows us to slow down long enough to think about the deeper things of life." Art and creativity are innate and primal forms of expression. Whether through the medium of song, dance, painting, poetry, or prose—art has forever helped us express and understand the human condition. According to L'Engle,

> The search for meaning is behind the telling of stories around tribal fires at night; behind the drawing of animals on the walls of caves; the singing of melodies of love in spring; and of the death of green in autumn. It is part of the deepest longing of the human psyche, a recurrent ache in the hearts of all of God's creatures.[19]

In his book *Unceasing Worship*, author and musician Harold Best comments on the unique language and vocabulary of the various art forms. He writes:

> Each art form has its own propositional mechanisms, its own particular kinds of language and vocabulary, and its own way of holding together in a final shape . . . As soon as we attempt to front-load an art form with a truth task of which it is incapable, we immediately call into question the mechanisms and expressive worth of the art forms themselves. Before we know it, the art form has begun to collapse, to cease being its inherent self, as it struggles to carry an illegitimate burden . . . all artists have an ethical obligation before God to be truthful in their reasons for making art as well as for bringing the interior truthfulness of all of their art to magnificent conclusion.[20]

Understanding the "propositional mechanisms," and "interior truthfulness" of various art forms is a vital consideration for understanding the role of artistic media. According to Best, "theological thought should provide mechanisms that validate the arts, distinguish among them, inform their use and direct them, according to their kind, in the continuing worship of God."[21]

Best's analysis is very insightful and challenges any serious student of both theology and the arts to listen and discern the unique function of each particular art form so that each one does not "struggle to carry an illegitimate burden." We should give serious attention to the unique way that each art form can *appropriately* serve the Christian meta-narrative. Whether through story, image, lyrical or poetic language, much of the power of art lies in its ability to open our eyes to meaning and truth.

A Biblical Survey of Artistic Media

The prescriptions for the temple. We will begin our biblical survey by exploring the prescriptions for the temple. In an article entitled, "The Divine Obsession: God's Preoccupation with Beauty," worship leader Jonathan Gilley cites some interesting facts about the "blueprints" for the Temple that the people of Israel were to build. Gilley first notes, "It almost makes us uncomfortable to see the lavish, costly, and beautiful materials that God prescribed to be used in its construction."[22]

He then goes on to describe two Bronze Pillars that were erected directly at the entrance to the Temple. Rising fifty-two feet high, he notes, "these were huge, massive columns. The amount of bronze used was 'more than could be weighed.'" The striking thing, Gilley notes, is that "They served no functional purpose!" These massive columns containing more bronze than could be weighed were strictly freestanding and non-load bearing, as they did not support a roof or any other structure. Gilley states, "They were there only for the aesthetic beauty they provided." Citing the robes worn by the priests, Gilley describes how they were prescribed by God to be hemmed with the likeness of pomegranates by using yarn of "blue, purple, and scarlet." "The amazing thing to note," says Gilley, "is that pomegranates can, at various degrees of ripeness, be purple or scarlet, however, at no time will they ever be blue." He concludes that we see the God of the universe "creating abstract art based on something he has already created!"[23]

Gilley summarizes the purpose of citing these examples in the following statement:

> There are surely many more deep theological implications which we can learn from all of this, however, it does not imply less than this: God loves beauty—it is extremely important to him.[24]

This is an important statement, for it challenges us to truly study the whole of biblical revelation and discover all of the "theological implications" of the role of art and beauty—which are clearly attributes of our Creator-God. In relation to God's own love of beauty, art, and creativity, I would borrow the words of C. S. Lewis and conclude that "Our Lord finds our desires, not too strong, but too weak."[25]

The story of Nathan and David. The story of Nathan and David, found in 2 Samuel 12, has powerful implications for understanding the intersection of worship, art, and gospel.

> The LORD sent Nathan to David. When he came to him, he said, "There were two men in a certain town, one rich and the other poor. The rich man had a very large number of sheep and cattle, but the poor man had nothing except one little ewe lamb he had bought. He raised it, and it grew up with him and his children. It shared his food, drank from his cup and even slept in his arms. It was like a daughter to him.
>
> "Now a traveler came to the rich man, but the rich man refrained from taking one of his own sheep or cattle to prepare a meal for the traveler who had come to him. Instead, he took the ewe lamb that belonged to the poor man and prepared it for the one who had come to him."
>
> David burned with anger against the man and said to Nathan, "As surely as the LORD lives, the man who did this deserves to die! He must pay for that lamb four times over, because he did such a thing and had no pity."
>
> Then Nathan said to David, "You are the man!" (2 Samuel 12:1-7a)

In his book, *The Doctrine of the Knowledge of God,* and in his lectures on ethics, Frame introduced the concept of "seeing" and "seeing as"—knowing something intellectually, yet not grasping it with your heart. Frame describes this concept by using David's sin with Bathsheba as an example. Frame demonstrates how David knew the Scriptures; he knew adultery and murder were wrong; yet somehow, the moral dimension of his acts was missed (he didn't "see as").[26]

Frame concludes that "Perhaps, he had rationalized; perhaps, he was spiritually cold." Thus, when Nathan confronted David (2 Sam. 12) he revealed, in a sense, no new facts to David—neither facts about Scripture nor facts about his actions. "Rather," Frame points out, "he put the facts already known into a pattern which presented obvious analogies with Scripture. The parable of the ewe lamb shocked David into seeing the pattern with full clarity."[27] It is interesting to note that David poured out his famous lament in Psalm 51 after this encounter with Nathan. David's repentance in this Psalm reveals that he was finally able to see his sin with the eyes of his heart.

According to Frame, "ethical discourse is never merely a matter of setting forth facts and verses." He concludes that "it may sometimes be useful, not only to reason, but also to tell stories, to pray, to sing, to share analogies, to do odd things for 'shock value' (Ezekiel), to teach by example."[28]

These conclusions are vital for connecting art and gospel, understanding and illumination. "Seeing" is not the same as "seeing as." Knowing something *intellectually* is not the same as knowing something *spiritually* in your heart. Certainly, artistry and nuance play roles in discerning between the two. The story of Nathan and David is one of many such examples where artistic means have been used to open the eyes of God's people.

The ministry of the prophets. The Prophets also reveal the use of artistry in order to open the eyes of the people of God. The prophets use as their tools rich language and marvelous metaphors, "the language of the imagination," according to Michael Card, contemporary scholar and musician.[29] He writes:

> Isaiah speaks of the sun and moon being ashamed; the trees clap their hands. God is seen as a Rock. In the prophets we also see God speaking through the bizarre activities of the prophets that called for an extra measure of obedience. Jeremiah hides his linen belt (Jer. 13). He breaks the clay jar (Jer. 19). Ezekiel constructs a toy town in the dust (Eze. 4). Hosea knowingly marries a prostitute (Hos. 1:2). The list goes on and on.[30]

Each of these citations is an example of how God opens the eyes of our hearts. Just as Frame used the story of Nathan confronting David, Card demonstrates how the prophets, too, utilized every day objects, architecture, shock value, and real-life metaphors to help God's people to see things from a spiritual perspective.

Old Testament theologian Willem VanGemeren writes:

> The prophetic speech is poetic, imaginative, full of similes and metaphors. It is the language of pictures and windows, drawn from the cultural context of the day. Through his servants, the prophets, God the Father pulled back the curtain of the new age and allowed his children, before and after Christ, to grasp a little of the glory prepared for them.[31]

In his book, *Interpreting the Prophetic Word*, VanGemeren describes how the interpreter of the prophets must be sensitive to their historical context as well as their language and literary imagery. He teaches that the prophets received a vision of God but spoke of it in a language that people could understand. In VanGemeren's words, "The prophets painted multi-faceted pictures representing the acts of God from their days until the full inauguration of the kingdom of God." They were "communicators of the word . . . poets with a message," who "creatively used Israel's cultural and revelatory heritage."[32]   According to Card:

> Being the Creator-Artist that he is, the Great Romancer, the perfectly loving Father, God calls out to us, sings to us, paints images in our minds through the prophets' visions. These sounds and songs, these visions, stand at the door of our imaginations and knock. Through them God opens the door of his own inner life to us . . . He pleads for us to open the eyes of our hearts, to hear with our ears, to really understand.[33]

One might argue that these methods were used in the Old Testament, but they do not apply to us today. To this argument Card offers a response:

> We can apply this understanding to our own creative efforts at many levels. On the most superficial level, we learn from the prophets that the tools best suited for communicating to the imagination are images, parables and sometimes even bizarre activity! At a deeper level, we learn that if we are to effect a permanent change in people's hearts, we must do more than simply teach them facts or reduce them to some emotional experience. Like the prophets, we must learn to reach out to the heart as well as the mind by speaking to the imagination.[34]

Having explored the role of artistic media in the Old Testament, we will now look through the pages of the New Testament and discover how Jesus, himself, employed artistic means of communication.

The life of Jesus. Jesus is the word made flesh. Through Christ God made his dwelling among us. Understanding the way in which God the Son communicated to the people of his day is of great cultural and theological significance. In *The New Testament: Its Background, Growth, and Content,* Bruce Metzger writes:

> Before analyzing some of the leading ideas of Jesus' teaching, it is necessary to examine the literary form in which that teaching was communicated. In such an examination the question to be asked is not what Jesus said, but how he said it. More than once it will be found that the meaning of his teaching is conditioned by the literary forms in which he expressed himself.[35]

Metzger lists the following forms of Jesus' teaching: picturesque speech (Matt. 7:3-5), puns (John 3:8), proverbs (Matt. 7:1; 7:6), poetry (Luke 6:27-28; 9:48; 17:26-30; Mark 8:35), and parables (Luke 10:29-37; Matt. 20:1-16). Metzger states that in all the teaching of Jesus "there is no feature more striking than his parables."[36] In accord with Paul's prayer to the Ephesians, Metzger concludes:

> Taken all together Jesus' parables were governed by a single pur-
> pose—to show directly, or indirectly, what God is and what man
> may become, and to show these things in such a way that they will
> reach men's hearts if it is possible to reach them at all.[37]

John 8 provides an enlightening example of how Jesus utilized dramatic gestures to make a point. When confronted with a woman caught in adultery, Jesus did not offer an immediate response; rather, he did something unexpected. He knelt down and began to scribble in the sand. Reflecting on the passage Card writes:

> What Jesus did that morning created a space in time that allowed
> the angry mob first to cool down, then to hear his word, and finally
> to think about it, be convicted by it and respond—or not. It made
> time stand still. It was original. It was unexpected . . . Jesus' action
> created a frame around the silence—the kind of silence in which
> God speaks to the heart. In short, it was a supreme act of creativity.
> It was art.[38]

Milne remarks that though "ingenious suggestions" have been made as to what Jesus might have been writing, "Certainly it was a dramatic gesture which would have heightened considerably the tension of the moment."[39] Hendriksen notes that Jesus "remained silent, simply scribbling figures or letters in the sand," concluding, however, "This was a silence that spoke louder than words."[40] Thus, Jesus' own life reflects a desire to help people see with the eyes of their heart. Through the use of words (picturesque speech, poetry, parable) and silence, Jesus demonstrates the power of literary art forms and dramatic gestures to teach the people of God—to create space for them to wrestle with the truth about God and themselves.

Just like those in the Old Testament and those who walked with Jesus, we need art forms to speak to our imagination; to open our eyes to the meaning of God's word for our lives. In an article on the arts in worship, worship leader and musician Tom Jennings writes:

> The gospel teaches us that Christianity is not only the acceptance of
> a body of truth, but it is the igniting of those truths in our hearts
> through a relationship with Jesus. And this is where the arts are

most useful . . . Intellectually, one may accept that God created man in His image, but may never weep over that truth until being overwhelmed by Michaelangelo's ceiling fresco in the Sistine Chapel in Rome depicting the hand of God breathing life into Adam . . . The church needs intelligent and beautiful expressions of art so that we can more fully grasp the gospel.[41]

The Artistic Media of Worship

The idea for this book began with a question that was raised one day in the context of a seminary course on contemporary models of worship. The question was, "Is worship art?" Given such a question, some will instinctively respond negatively, arguing that worship is for the glory of God alone; or, by deferring to the second commandment, insisting that anything considered "art" in worship is prohibited. Indeed, for some, associating the words worship and art may conjure only negative connotations. Still, others may find great delight and satisfaction in the idea of worship as art and may naively find license in bringing creative ideas into worship that may not have biblical warrant. Yet, for many others, when asked to consider this question, the answer is simply not clear. The question is approached with wisdom and prudence, seeking biblical guidance, while avoiding blind traditionalism. I remember we had quite a lively dialogue that day in class, but never came to any dogmatic conclusions.

To be sure, the primary purpose of corporate worship is for the glory of God—it has a vertical focus and aim. However, we can also speak of the secondary aims of worship recognizing that there is a horizontal dimension as well. Worship is offered *by* God's people, *through* various means, including: the ministry of the word, the observance of the sacraments, and the expression of songs, prayers, and professions of faith. Thus, while I'm hesitant to say that worship *is* art, I would say that worship incorporates *artistic media* of expression—story, imagery and experience, lyrical and poetic expression. Each of these media, in fact, reflects the different perspectives of worship that we will explore in the remainder of this book.

Moreover, in a very powerful way, these different perspectives of corporate worship create not a vicarious experience, but a *present reality*. The worshipper plays not the role of mere observer, but that of *active participant*. Through the ministry of the word, worshippers do not just recount a story, we find ourselves *in* the story as part of the unfolding drama of redemption. Through the sacraments, we do not passively observe framed images; we get to experientially touch them, feel them, taste them, indeed, drink them down to the last drop! Through song, prayer, and profession we do not merely listen to the words of another, we lift up our *own* voices through the gift of music, the intimacy of prayer, and the heritage of truth.

Finally, while this book handles many biblical and theological issues, its ultimate aim is pastoral in nature. Exploring the intersection of gospel, art, and worship is for the purpose of better understanding the craft of worship planning which directly affects the people of God each and every Lord's Day. There is a high level of responsibility placed on those crafting liturgies—those seeking to create space and opportunity for worshippers to have an encounter with God and a clear and relevant communication of the gospel. Thus, in addition to being students of theology and artistic media, it is important that worship planners see themselves as shepherds of the flock.

Articulating foundational qualifications for the worship leader, Wade Williams, an experienced worship leader in the Presbyterian Church in America, writes:

> The worship leader must have a pastor's heart for the people he is ministering to . . . He should be viewed more as a priest than a prophet (taking the people's prayers and praises to God, and using liturgy, prayer and song, bringing God's encouragement to the people).[42]

As worship planners we serve as "priests" and facilitators of God's encounter with his people. Thus, we must be intentional about everything we do, for through this craft there is the opportunity to enrich and edify the spiritual lives of God's people—to open our eyes to the beauty of the gospel through the artistic media of the story, imagery, and expression. Such gospel-centered worship begins, in part, with the lives of hungry and thirsty gospel-centered worship leaders.

NOTES

1. John M. Frame, *The Doctrine of the Knowledge of God* (Phillipsburg, N.J.: Presbyterian and Reformed, 1987) 89.
2. Ibid., 90.
3. John M. Frame, *The Doctrine of God* (Phillipsburg, N.J.: Presbyterian and Reformed, 2002) 15–16.

4. Frame, *The Doctrine of the Knowledge of God*, 74–75.

5. Richard L. Pratt Jr. *He Gave Us Stories* (Phillipsburg, N.J.: Presbyterian and Reformed, 1990) 1.

6. Dallas Willard, *The Divine Conspiracy* (New York: HarpersCollins, 1998) xiii.

7. *Fellowship Group Handbook* (Redeemer Presbyterian Church, 1997) 1–2.

8. John R.W. Stott, *The Message of Ephesians* (Downers Grove: InterVarsity, 1979), 54.

9. William Hendriksen, *The Epistle to the Ephesians* (Grand Rapids: Baker, 1967) 98.

10. Stott, *Ephesians*, 53–54.

11. Morna D. Hooker, *Not Ashamed of the Gospel: New Testament Interpretations of the Death of Christ* (Paternoster, 1994) 8.

12. Derek Tidball, *The Message of the Cross* (Downers Grove, Ill.: InterVarsity, 2001) 200.

13. John R. W. Stott, *The Cross of Christ* (Downers Grove, Ill.: InterVarsity, 1986) 225.

14. Tidball, *The Message of the Cross*, 209.

15. Scotty Smith, *Objects of His Affection* (West Monroe, La.: Howard, 2001) 1.

16. Ibid., 29.

17. Quote from Gregory Wolfe shared in a seminary lecture.

18. Chuck Smith Jr. "A Taste of Heaven," *Worship Leader* 12 (January/February 2003) 24.

19. Madeleine L'Engle, *Walking On Water* (Colorado Springs: Waterbrook, 1980) 3.

20. Harold M. Best, *Unceasing Worship* (Downers Grove, Ill.: InterVarsity, 2003) 157.

21. Ibid., 160.

22. Jonathan Gilley, "The Divine Obsession: God's Preoccupation with Beauty" (unpublished article, 2002) 1.

23. Ibid.

24. Ibid.

25. C. S. Lewis, "The Weight of Glory," in *The Weight of Glory and other Essays* (Grand Rapids: Eerdmans, 1965) 1–2.

26. John M. Frame, "Pastoral and Social Ethics," lecture notes, 106–7.

27. Ibid.

28. Ibid.

29. Michael Card, *Scribbling in the Sand* (Downers Grove, Ill.: InterVarsity, 2002) 60.

30. Ibid.

31. Willem A. VanGemeren, *Interpreting the Prophetic Word* (Grand Rapids: Zondervan, 1990) 73.

32. Ibid., 76.

33. Card, *Scribbling*, 59.

34. Ibid., 60–61.

35. Bruce M. Metzger, *The New Testament: Its Background, Growth, and Content* (Nashville: Abingdon, 1983) 136.

36. Ibid., 141.

37. Ibid., 142.

38. Card, *Scribbling*, 16.

39. Bruce Milne, *The Message of John* (Downers Grove, Ill.: InterVarsity, 1993) 125.

40. William Hendriksen, *Exposition of the Gospel According to John, Volume II* (Grand Rapids: Baker, 1953) 38.

41. Tom Jennings, "The Arts in Worship" (lecture notes on worship, Redeemer Presbyterian Church, New York, NY).
42. Wade Williams, "Christian Worship and Music," lecture notes, 42.

PART 1

Cultivating Gospel-Centered Worship Leaders

In the first part of this book we will explore worship from the *existential perspective*, emphasizing personal and professional issues by focusing on the worship leader—the one who will, for the most part, be planning and crafting worship. In Chapter One we will focus on the *interior* dimensions of the worship leader, one's life and community. We will discuss the unique identity of every worship leader and the necessity of gospel-centered staff relationships, small group relationships and peer mentoring. In Chapter Two we will discuss the *exterior* dimensions of the worship leader, exploring various ministry qualifications and kingdom investments.

1

The Life and Community of the Worship Leader

ON DECEMBER 29, 1997—one week before I was to begin my first full-time position as a worship leader at a church in Florida—I suffered a severe injury, severing nerves, tendons, and an artery in the palm of my right hand. I spent five and a half hours in microscopic surgery, seven a half weeks in occupational therapy, and many, many nights crying out to God (much like Asaph in Psalm 77), wondering if I would ever play the guitar again. God did restore the use of my hand—though I had to adapt my playing style quite a bit—and in February of 1998 I drove down to Florida to continue my calling as a worship leader.

The Unique Identity of the Worship Leader

I share this because every one of us has a story; every worship leader has a unique story. Worship leaders don't roll off an assembly line, armed and ready to facilitate the worship of God's people. Each comes with a unique "back story" of events, dreams, trials, and circumstances that has shaped (and will shape) who God has made them to be; and therefore, the worship leader whom God calls to a local body will be one factor in shaping the worship identity of that church.

In his book, *The Doctrine of the Knowledge of God,* Professor Frame includes a very important section entitled: "The Existential Perspective - The Qualifications of the Theologian." In this section he describes the "personal" nature of doing theology:

> Theology is the expression and application of a person's deepest convictions, his presuppositions. Therefore it is inevitable that in his work the theologian shares *himself* with his readers at a level of some intimacy.[1]

This is a very important point, not only in the area of theology, but also in the area of worship. In the next two chapters we will focus on the life and ministry of the worship leader as a person—the one who plans and facilitates various facets of a gospel-centered worship ministry. The worship leader is a key player in fleshing out a gospel-centered worship theology in the context of a worshipping community.

I will never forget two words shared by a close friend just before I took my first full-time worship position, "Be you." It is important to acknowledge the unique qualities of a given worship leader and how they will help shape the character of a local congregation. These qualities can be broken down into three major categories: personal life, spiritual life, and professional life.

Please note that I am not trying to imply that these descriptions are independent of one another; however, for the sake of clarity and discussion, I will discuss them separately—even though in reality, they are intimately connected.

Personal Life

When I received a guitar for my twelfth birthday it more took hold of me than I took hold of it. I resonate with the words of Eric Little from the movie *Chariots of Fire* when he said, "When I run, I feel his pleasure." For me, playing the guitar came naturally, and from the very beginning, provided me with a sense of identity and calling. I would play scales up and down the fretboard for hours, both to become as fast and proficient as Eddie Van Halen (I did not fully succeed!) and to drown out the noise of my mom and older sister who would often be arguing in another room.

I think it is important and helpful for a congregation to know the story of their leaders. I will often share my testimony during a portion of our New Members class. I also think church staff members should share their stories with one another. Worship leaders may better appreciate their pastors who are transparent and willing to share stories of failure, grief, and loss. Pastors might better understand their worship leaders when they discover how their craft was learned or the context of their home life.

Is a given worship leader married or single? Does he have children? What kind of hobbies does he enjoy? What kind of background and family life did he experience? These are questions that will help shed light on the personal trials and struggles one will or has faced. These are questions that are just as important to one's "success" as one's skill level and talent.

My parents got divorced when I was eight years old. I lived with my mom and sister for much of my childhood and adolescence, visiting my

Dad every other weekend. I suffered a tragic and devastating hand injury at the age of 25. I was raised in the South. These are pieces of my story that have shaped who I am. They make me, in part, the worship leader I am today—with various accompanying strengths and weaknesses. Yet, as the psalmist acknowledges: "I praise you because I am fearfully and wonderfully made . . . All the days ordained for me were written in your book before one of them came to be" (Psalm 139:14, 16).

We claim this verse for every child of God and, for sure, every worship leader. Our personal life, our family history, our own unique story is simply part of who we are as God's instruments—part of his redemptive plan to work "all things for the good of those who love him, who have been called according to his purpose" (Romans 8:28).

Professional Life

I can readily identify six worship leader friends with whom I enjoy some degree of regular fellowship:

1) A piano oriented worship leader with a sacred music degree and a lot of talent, heart, and charisma.

2) A jazz-style bass player—short on words, but deep in musicianship and professionalism—who leads with nodds and cues.

3) A trained theologian and musician who plays, primarily, saxophone.

4) A classically trained vocalist who now functions mostly as a vocal-oriented worship leader, but who also directs a choir and leads with guitar on occasion or when needed.

5) A studied guitar player who loves to write charts and who leads with a more laid-back style, yet with an understated passion.

6) A classically trained "organist-turned-contemporary-style" worship leader.

27

These worship leaders all differ in their musical and leadership style as well as their training; yet they all share one very important thing in common: they all believe deeply in the power of the gospel.

These descriptions reveal the fact that there is no "one-size-fits-all" worship leader. Each comes with a unique blend of strengths and weaknesses; yet, the most important quality is that a given worship leader really believes in the power of the gospel. Musicians and artists often struggle with the conflicts that characterize the personal and subjective nature of their profession. How one deals with these issues reveals how well one understands and is able to apply the gospel.

Rory Noland's book, *The Heart of the Artist*, deals head-on with the many issues that are a regular part of any artist's life: servanthood versus stardom, excellence versus perfectionism, jealousy and envy, handling criticism. These are all very common idols and emotions for artists. As an attempt to handle many of the above issues that plague the members of my worship and arts ministry, I have spent some time leading us through these various topics. We have talked about what it looks like to be a servant rather than striving for stardom; how to be content with the gifts God has given us and not always comparing ourselves with others. These inner conflicts can eat away at us. And often, these professional conflicts are intimately connected with one's spiritual life. These conflicts and emotions (jealousy, envy, criticism, comparing, seeking stardom) affect our spiritual lives and can likely lead to very unhealthy means of coping with disappointment, frustration, and despair.

Spiritual Life

We don't intuitively connect jealousy, envy, and criticism with worship, but idolatry is at the very heart of these emotions and the various forms of escape to which we often turn. It is very important to first be honest and recognize the professional conflicts that plague us, but then we have to go a step further and see how these become very spiritual issues. It is vital that we understand that *how we respond to the struggles and hard seasons of life reveals what we are truly choosing to worship.*

Cultivating the Heart of the Psalmist

I don't remember when the phrase, "cultivating the heart of the psalmist," first began to resonate with me, but now I cannot escape it. It has taken up permanent residence in my soul and describes, to a large extent, the trajectory I desire in my walk with the Lord. I have always felt a kindred spirit with the psalmists. Their brutal honesty about life and their bold conversations with the Lord make me jealous for such relational dynamics in my own walk.

Thus, I have begun writing on a series of topics, seeking to connect the dots between worship and all of the "stuff" of life that we deal with Monday through Saturday: addictions, stardom, doubt, discontentment, etc. These are issues that every worship leader faces and it is vitally important that one is in touch with these interior issues, the landscape of one's heart.

Ironically, my first year in full-time ministry was filled with a deep sense of loneliness, a burdening sense of inadequacy, a naïve understanding of people and church politics, and an unhealthy need of approval. All of this combined with a traumatic and devastating hand injury, a long distance relationship, and no real sense community often led me down a path of learning how to numb my pain and escape from my circumstances. So often I had a real choice before me: I could either choose to find satisfaction in God alone, or turn to something else for comfort.

Unfortunately, I often chose the idol of escape. The sad thing is that, most of the time, I wasn't in touch with the emotional landscape of my heart enough to know why I felt so restless; nor did I have a biblical language to meet me in my restlessness. And, quite frankly, I simply did not want to sit in my pain long enough to find the voice of God; yet, it is precisely in the hour of loneliness, pain, and despair that the psalmists turn their gaze toward God.

From the darkest of lament to the most exuberant of praise, the Psalms portray the lyrical record of lives lived in perpetual response to God. In the Psalms we find a vocabulary strong enough to articulate our deepest desires and emotions. Through the Psalms we can learn how to express ourselves honestly, but healthily, in the midst of the various circumstances of life. This is what it means to cultivate the heart of the psalmist: not turning from our pain, but diving directly into it - learning to express our true feelings, in all of life, whether praise or lament, doubt or adoration, joy or tears.

The following are some areas of life and important questions to which every worship leader (indeed, every Christian!) must respond.

Worship and Compartmentalized Christianity (Psalm 139)

How do I live the rest of the week?

Often, in our walk, we think we can live outside of the presence of God. Even though, intellectually, we know we can't hide from God; functionally, we fool ourselves and act as if we can. But the psalmist reminds us, "You discern my going out and my lying down; you are familiar with all my ways" (Psalm 139:3). Acts of worship are not confined to an hour on Sunday. In one sense, all of life is worship. The problem is we're not always worshipping the one true God. We often choose to worship idols rather than the Lord. We will bow to the idols of comfort and success, fortune and fame. We can easily compartmentalize worshipping God to a particular time, or place, or set of actions that we do; but worship is a 24/7 way of life. Everything we do is done before the Lord, either exalting *him* or ourselves.

Worship and Ambition (Psalm 27)

What is my deepest desire?

The psalmist writes, "One thing I ask of the Lord, this is what I seek: that I may dwell in the house of the Lord all the days of my life, to gaze upon the beauty of the Lord and to seek him in his temple" (Psalm 27:4). The deepest desire of the psalmist is made clear: to dwell in the presence of the Lord and gaze upon his beauty. I have to confess, this is not always my deepest desire. My desires are all too often tainted with selfish ambition. It's not always black and white—most of the time I have Godly motives, but they are mixed with a desire for personal success. I often ask the Lord to purify my motives and give me an "undivided heart."

Worship and Stardom (Psalm 96)

Who do I really want to receive all the glory?

As a worship leader I have been influenced by people like Andy Park and Brian Doerksen (gifted worship leader/songwriters). At times, however, part of me has wanted to be *like* them (i.e., to be "known" and "famous" like them). Again, like ambition, this isn't my only desire. I really do want to bring glory to God, but I also wrestle with wanting to make a name for myself.

Psalm 96 offers the following exhortation: "Ascribe to the Lord, O families of nations, ascribe to the Lord glory and strength. Ascribe to the Lord the glory due his name" (Psalm 96:7-8). The only name we should be making famous is the Lord's. He is the only one worthy of praise. His name is the name above all names—the name to which every knee will bow and every tongue confess as Lord. Worship *is* about stardom . . . it's just not about ours! It's about making God's name famous among the nations.

Worship and Lamentation (Psalm 42)

Where do I go with my doubts, my pain, and my anger?

It's extremely comforting that the psalmists often cried out in their times of doubt, pain, and anger. I am grateful for the words of the psalmist, wondering, "Why are you downcast, O my soul? Why so disturbed within me? Put your hope in God, for I will yet praise him, my Savior and my God" (Psalm 42:5).

I am so thankful for the psalms of lament for they give me language for the hard, almost unbearable seasons of life. I shared earlier of how my first full-time position as a worship leader was a very trying season—one filled with loneliness, feelings of inadequacy, and the trauma of a devastating hand injury. These seasons really expose the landscape of our hearts—our false idols, patterns of escape, and unhealthy means of coping with the harsh realities of life.

During these seasons it is so important to learn how to linger in our pain before trying to simply numb it, avoid it, or pretend that it's not there. The psalmists knew how to "vent" their emotions, but then pivot into praise by remembering and recalling the character of God—his faithfulness, his unfailing love, the years of his "right hand." It can be a very sweet and intimate season of our journey when we learn how to worship in the very midst of lamentation.

Worship and Addictions (Psalm 77)

How do I cope with the highs and lows of life?

In a very blunt and honest conversation with a worship leader friend one day, I realized that learned patterns of behavior can be both ways of *coping* with the lows and, though distorted, *celebrating* the highs of life. For those wrestling with serious addictions I would exhort you to confide in someone, share your struggles, and come out from hiding. Living a double-life will destroy you. Like the psalmist, "In the day of . . . trouble . . . seek the Lord" (Psalm 77:2). Wrestle with him, cry out to him—he can handle it! Pray that you might turn from the dark and destructive patterns of addiction and remember the deeds of the Lord. Like the psalmist, we have to fill our minds with the character and mighty acts of God.

Worship and Discontentment (Psalm 73)

Why does the grass always seem greener on the other side?

In our sinful nature we are often looking around the corner for the next thing: a new home, a better job. Worship involves resting in God—learning, simply, how to be content. The psalmist acknowledged that in his discontentment, in his bitterness towards and envy of others, he was "like a beast" toward God. After many verses of venting, he finally comes to the conclusion that there is "nothing on earth I desire besides you" (Psalm 73:25).

Realizing this truth at a deep level will bring about real contentment. No amount of money or success or comfort in this life will bring us the contentment that our souls so desperately desire. Only God can bring us the rest and contentment we truly desire. He, alone, truly satisfies. Augustine writes: "You stir man to take pleasure in praising you, because you have made us for yourself, and our heart is restless until it rests in you."[2]

Cultivating the heart of the psalmist is not a step-by-step program. It is about a dynamic relationship. It is learning, simply, how to walk with God through the highs and lows of life; how to carry on a bold and intimate conversation with him; how to worship him through all of the various seasons of life, with an awareness of his presence every moment of every day.

Of course, God never intended for us to deal with life alone. In the next section I will discuss the importance of gospel community and how this relational and edifying dynamic can also help us work through various trials and struggles in community together.

The Necessity of Gospel Community

Gospel-Centered Staff Relationships

In Chapter Eight I will discuss the importance of having a comprehensive vision for gospel community. This is vital for creating a context for gospel-centered worship. Staff relationships should be characterized by a growing sense of trust, openness, honesty, confrontation, and love. The worship leader and youth minister should not be add odds with one another; the children's minister should not feel that he or she has to walk on egg shells around the worship leader. Conflicts will inevitably arise. I am not suggesting that your church staff should reflect some kind of fictional, utopian society; however, I am suggesting that people should not gossip, hold grudges, harbor jealousy and envy, or withhold opinions. Church staffs should strive for mutual encouragement and edification, all in a professional, gospel-centered environment. This dynamic must come from the top down. For this kind of atmosphere to prevail, the governing body of the church, as well as the senior pastor, must first model it.

Small Group Relationships

Another important dimension of community for the worship leader is a small group in which to study and apply the word, experience kingdom-centered prayer, and share personal struggles and trials. Particularly if a given worship leader is single, the value of having a small group for regular bible study, prayer, and accountability cannot be overstated. It is all too easy for any ministry leader to lead a dual life: leading one lifestyle in one's professional life, yet leading a very different lifestyle in one's personal life.

Most ministry leaders do not fall because of poor time-management skills or because of a lack of talent. Most people in ministry fall because they have led a dual lifestyle, hiding and managing sinful patterns that eventually come to light. Having a small group community with whom to share life is a huge step forward in revealing who we really are to others; and thus, helping break down the destructive pattern of a dual lifestyle.

Often, when a worship leader is hired by a church, that individual or couple must relocate to take the new position. Having a small group community is also vital for feeling connected to a new community.

Peer Mentoring

In addition to having healthy, gospel-centered staff relationships and an intimate small group community, it is also important for a worship leader to have some significant relationships with others of the same profession. Having the freedom and context in which to share personal and professional issues with other worship leaders is a third and final consideration in this discussion of community dynamics.

In life there are often opportunities to mentor in a variety of directions. When we think of mentoring relationships we usually think of the *vertical* dynamic: either having someone "above" us or "below" us. But mentoring also has a *horizontal* dynamic: we mentor one another as peers.

This is a vital aspect of mentoring and a dynamic I have learned to value at a deep level.

A few years ago a worship leader within my particular denomination gathered some of his peers together, informally, capitalizing on a worship conference that would be bringing them to the same city. This was a simple gesture, flowing from the heart of one worship leader, to gather some friends and share community together. It has blossomed into a network with an executive committee, a steering committee, and associate members.

We have met more officially on several occasions as a steering committee; have played a role in planning and facilitating a national conference on worship; and have formed an internet group of nearly three hundred members, regularly discussing various topics on worship and liturgy. Of all the various dynamics that this network has enjoyed, however, the dynamic of "peer mentoring" has been one of both great surprise and exhilaration.

I use the word "surprise" because many of us (virtually all of us) had never before enjoyed such rich, honest, and mutually edifying relationships with other worship leaders. We had simply been so consumed with our own churches and ministries that we never had the forum to share the issues near to our heart with other people in the same profession. Many of us felt an immediate bond simply because we "live in the same world." We deal with the same joys and struggles on a daily, weekly, and annual basis.

Creating this network also invited me into a more intimate relationship with some other worship leaders with whom I had related to at some level, but not to the extent that we now share. We have revealed issues of a very personal and spiritual nature that simply could not be shared with the same level of understanding and empathy with anyone else.

It is exhilarating to pray at a deep level with other peers, interceding for one another and for our congregations; crying out to God for a desire to seek him above all else; for hearts and minds that would believe the gospel at a deep level; for the dismantling of the idols of success, recognition, glory, and fame; for victory over besetting sins; for purity in our marriages. It doesn't get much better than this. When ministry leaders form networks with one another, lifting their hearts together in prayer, I can't help but think that God is smiling.

Finally, peer mentoring also helps sharpen worship leaders, professionally. Whenever I get together with peers either to play together or share resources, I always learn something new. I always come away with something that I can try out in my own setting and context. I always come away feeling inspired and refreshed. At the very least, I come away with a new song to introduce to my own congregation.

We can tend to become a bit isolated, on the one hand working under the prideful assumption that we really have all the resources we need. On the other hand, we can operate out of the fearful assumption that others are much more skilled than we; that we don't have anything to contribute; that our songs aren't all that good and, thus, remain too intimidated to rub shoulders and interact with other worship leaders.

This is simply the result of not applying gospel principles to our relationships with our professional peers. The gospel tells us to find our identity in Christ alone. Thinking either too highly of ourselves, or too little of ourselves keeps us from gospel-humility on the one hand, and gospel-boldness on the other. When we are resting in Christ, we can humbly learn from others and boldly share with others at the same time.

I want to close this chapter with the testimony of a close worship leader friend, Phil Mershon. Phil recently wrote about his first year "in the trenches" as a worship leader in suburban Chicago. Phil shares about his experience in a church-planting situation; however his thoughts have universal application.

> As I have entered this spiritual ministry, I've made the mistake of thinking of this as just a job. This is a calling and a ministry. As such, it needs to be bathed in prayer and fasting. I'm learning to expect spiritual warfare. It will come from within and without. Relationships with musicians can be extremely painful. One of my hardest times came through dealing with a Christian band member who, while extraordinarily talented and bright, struggled to follow my leadership. You never know where the enemy will strike. You can be almost certain that it will happen on Saturday night or Sunday morning. Make sure your prayer team is praying for you at the critical junctures in your week. In addition, don't forget to feed your own soul, even as your primary task is to feed the souls of others.
>
> St. John of the Cross penned a phrase, the "dark night of the soul." This is an apt definition of bitter loneliness. You might call it depression, anxiety or a prolonged case of indigestion, but you can expect it to come. The question is not "if," but "when." When the discouragement and loneliness settle in like a dark cloud, where will you turn? You need some friends around the country that you can call and with whom you can bear your soul. You need a safe place where you can take off your armor and share what's really going on. You need to find some solitary places of refuge where you can go in the figurative (and literal) cold of winter. My own experience has remarkably mirrored the seasons of the year. My "dark night" came in the cold of winter on one of the longest nights of the year. I'm very thankful for some friends who

reached out to me and lifted up my arms when I could barely get out of bed.

Who are your "Ghostbusters"? In other words, when the gunfire is whistling past your ears and the battle is drawing close, who are your mentors and friends that you can call for prayer, advice, and a listening ear. Be proactive about calling these friends. You can do it before you need help. Or, when you really need help it will become much more expensive. I'm finding that these friendships are a lifeline. If I'm not opening up with them, on a weekly basis, things start to unravel.

There is perhaps no place where you will feel the effects of church planting more poignantly than in your family, and especially your marriage. Church planting is hard work. I have felt the physical, emotional and spiritual strain throughout the year. I can't imagine having ridden the roller coaster of this last year without Audrey as my partner and teammate. We have seen our regular prayer times and date nights ebb and flow, but are reminded of how critical a lifeline these are for our relationship with each other and God.

Under the pressure of church planting where you are stretched and pulled in many ways, it's easy to forget why you are here. Remind yourself frequently of God's call on your life. At times that is the only thing you can cling to! For me, I can see 25 years of preparation for this last year. At times I found myself doubting my gifting and calling for this frontline challenge, but God has frequently reminded me of his gifting and calling on my life. It's not about me feeling adequate, but about him showing himself to be adequate for my every need! Remember what is true! The enemy will do everything imaginable to discourage and distract you. God is your refuge and strength. God's word is your comfort. Remember Paul's words to the Philippians, "Finally, brothers, whatever is true, whatever is noble, whatever is right, whatever is pure, whatever is lovely, whatever is admirable—if anything is excellent or praiseworthy—think about such things." [Philippians 4:8]

It is so important for a worship leader to be in touch with one's interior life; to be living in community with other believers; and to be learning how to connect the dots between worship and all of the various seasons of life. In the next chapter will explore the more outward and exterior dimensions; namely, ministry qualifications and kingdom investments.

NOTES

1. John M. Frame, *The Doctrine of the Knowledge of God* (Phillipsburg, N.J.: Presbyterian and Reformed, 1987) 319.
2. Augustine, *Confessions* (New York: Oxford University Press, 1991) 3.

2

Ministry Qualifications
and Kingdom Investments

A CHURCH PLANTER recently asked me, "So what do you guys call yourselves these days?" He was only half-joking. If you were to look on various church websites you might find the following descriptions for the person in charge of worship: "Worship Leader," "Lead Worshipper," "Director of Worship," "Director of Music," "Director of Worship and Music," "Director of Worship and Arts," or "Chief Musician." The descriptions can become dizzying.[1]

Integrating the Various Roles of Worship Leadership

The role of the worship leader has evolved drastically over the past several decades. The above descriptions reveal this fact. In today's culture the local worship leader must be able to wear a variety of hats. No longer does a worship leader function simply as a song leader or choir director, removed from the overall planning and integration of themes and liturgical elements. In fact, the worship leader is often the one planning various elements of a worship service, leading those various elements, and shepherding the members of his worship team (and, possibly, a variety of people involved in an integrated worship and arts ministry). Thus, the worship leader must be equipped in a variety of disciplines. He must have a "palette" of gifts and resources.

Though a variety of different models exist, I believe the worship leader must be able to exemplify three broad characteristics. He must be able to: think like a theologian, labor like an artist, and shepherd like a pastor.

Thinking like a Theologian

A worship leader should be able to think like a theologian, meaning that he must be familiar with the language of systematic, biblical and historical theology. Having an integrated theological framework will go a long way in the area of worship planning and in building a sense of trust with one's staff and congregation.

SYSTEMATIC THEOLOGY

A basic knowledge of systematic theology will alleviate the potential for *randomness* in worship planning. Familiarity with the various loci within systematic theology provides one with categories in which to place various sermon topics, thus offering general worship themes. Once a worship leader has a general theme such as God's providence or the atoning work of Christ, he can give intentional and creative focus to selecting songs, prayers, and other elements of worship.

BIBLICAL THEOLOGY

Biblical theology provides one with a *redemptive-historical* perspective of the Bible. The Bible is not a textbook. One should read the Bible as the unfolding drama of God's redemption of mankind. Biblical theology demonstrates how this theme runs throughout the Old and New Testament writings. As a liturgist, the worship leader acts as a kind of storyteller, facilitating a gospel-dialogue within the context of worship. Biblical theology will help equip the worship leader in this particular role.

HISTORICAL THEOLOGY

Historical theology is important for worship leaders because it helps one understand how various doctrines have developed throughout church history. It offers a context for understanding pertinent practices such as baptism and the Lord's Supper.

Laboring like an Artist

A worship leader must be able to labor like an artist, meaning that he should feel comfortable in the world of creative ideas and creative people. Being able to think and work creatively will complement and enhance the overall ministry of the church in significant ways. One should be developing and refining skills in the following areas: musicianship, crafting and leading a worship service, writing charts and leading rehearsals, programming special services and events.

MUSICIANSHIP

A pleasant singing voice. The worship leader does not have to be the best musician in the band, vocally or instrumentally; however, he should have a pleasant singing voice and should be able to guide the congregation in song. It is also helpful if the worship leader can accompany himself with an instrument (e.g., guitar or piano).

Musical literacy. It is highly beneficial to have some background in music theory and aural skills. For example, knowing how to perform simple chord analysis on a hymn, being able to sight read or play a new melody on a piano—these are all very important skills to have as a worship leader. If one does not have formal training in music there are several ways to acquire some basic skills. The simplest way would be to purchase a set of Alfred's *Essentials of Music Theory* and either teach oneself or hire a mentor. Another option would be to take music theory and aural skills at a local college or university. Having some formal training will only make one more effective and more versatile as a worship leader.

Appreciation for many styles of music. It is important for a worship leader to be exposed to various genres and styles of music, not just those he prefers. It is easy to only listen and select music with which one is familiar, but this is neither a wise nor pastoral way to operate. A good worship leader will always be growing in his understanding and appreciation of various musical styles. This will also enhance one's musicianship.

Growing in one's knowledge of Christian hymnody. We have such a rich heritage as Christians. There is such a rich variety of music that has been sung throughout the ages, and thus, a good working philosophy is to embrace the best of the old and the best of the new. It is so important for a worship leader to be growing in his knowledge of traditional Christian hymnody as well as new songs written for worship.[2]

CRAFTING AND LEADING A WORSHIP SERVICE

Musical resources. As a worship leader, one must become resourceful, being able to locate music that conveys a broad range of themes, style, etc.

39

This process can become more focused and less random once one has a general theme (which is why a working knowledge of systematic and biblical theology is important). However, one must know where and how to locate such musical resources, pulling from the best of the old and the best of the new.

Scripture and prayers. The worship leader must always be careful to give worshippers a God-ward gaze; thus, at the beginning of a service, one should offer a view of God from the Scriptures. This is referred to as the Call to Worship.

Often, Psalm texts or passages from the Prophets are used to give worshippers a picture of God—his holiness (e.g., Isaiah 6) or his glory in creation (e.g., Psalm 19). The worship leader must also be able to find or craft prayers of confession. This can be a very powerful part of the liturgy, especially if the prayers are visceral in nature, honestly articulating the truth about our sinful nature and our need of God's redeeming grace.

Creeds and confessions. Creeds and confessions of faith are rich means of articulating various doctrines and the fundamental truths of the Christian faith in a succinct way. Ancient creeds and confessions also give us a sense of connection with believers throughout the ages, thus being "surrounded by a cloud of witnesses" (Hebrews 12:1).

Presentation skills (speaking, posture, dress, etc.). A worship leader does not have to be the most polished public speaker. However, it is important that a worship leader articulates himself clearly; that he does not mumble or talk too fast; and that he chooses his words carefully. Regarding dress, it is important for a worship leader to be reflective of his culture. Wearing a Hawaiian shirt and sandals in a highly professional culture may not be a good idea; however, this may be the perfect attire in a more tropical, coastal environment. A worship leader should be a student of his culture, making wise and pastoral decisions, while still maintaining his own style and identity.

Writing Charts and Leading Rehearsals

Writing Charts. Being familiar with notation software and being able to write charts is an invaluable skill as a worship leader. Worship team musicians will greatly appreciate, for example, clean, legible charts with clear repeats, endings, and key changes.

In addition, an arrangement of a song may not always be in a preferable key, or it may not have a preferable harmonization. Thus, being able to chart arrangements gives a worship leader a lot of creative and musical freedom. This skill also allows a worship leader to chart original songs and make them broadly accessible to his worship team.

Sharing the theme of the service. I have found that it is a good idea to share the overall theme of a particular worship service or worship event with the worship team. This will give the team orientation and will help everyone to better engage with the various Scripture readings, songs, and other elements of the service.

Working with vocalists. When a worship leader is working with a number of instrumentalists and vocalists it is best to rehearse with each separately, if possible. This way the vocalists can concentrate on their parts without having to sing over the drummer, for example.

During rehearsals I regularly articulate the need for vocalists to blend their voices together. I also try to make them aware of their expressions and presence in front of those they are leading in worship. I tell my vocalists over and over that they are to be "lead worshippers." In other words, the best way for them to draw others in is by being genuinely engaged in worship themselves.

Working with instrumentalists. In working with instrumentalists, a worship leader should try to educate himself in the instrumentalist's world. In other words, he should learn the musical language associated with a particular instrument. This will help, for example, when a worship leader wants to convey a particular groove to a drummer or a certain sound or style to a flute player.

PROGRAMMING SPECIAL SERVICES AND EVENTS

As a worship ministry grows and becomes more integrated, artistically, a worship leader will likely find himself planning events and services that involve a broad spectrum of ministry areas: drama, sound, lighting, music, aesthetics, etc. Programming integrated events is very exciting, but also very challenging. A worship leader will often find himself making decisions, brainstorming ideas, and spending money in areas that are, more than likely, beyond his realm of expertise. Christmas programs and outreach events are examples of things a worship leader may find himself planning.

Learning how to delegate responsibilities to the right people is a key part of being a programming director. At times a worship leader may not be the one "on stage," yet he will be coordinating all of the efforts and decisions behind the scenes. Having an integrated worship and arts ministry that meets regularly and that is growing in community together will allow one to adequately plan for and pull off major events. A worship leader will find that being part of a team of creative and talented people is a very rewarding experience.

Shepherding like a Pastor

Finally, a worship leader must be sensitive to his role as a shepherd. He must invest in the relational aspect of ministry with one's worship team members and with his congregation. He should be learning and growing in the following areas: pastoral care, wise counsel, and administration.

PASTORAL CARE

Caring for oneself. A worship leader should always make sure that he is being refreshed spiritually. One crucial lesson I learned early on was the value of a day off. Without down time one will burn out. I like going to movies, running, or getting outdoors with my camera. These are things that get me away from the office and help restock the spiritual pond.

Though it's rare, I have also found that it is very healthy for me to attend a worship service that I do not have to lead! It is so refreshing to be able to sit in the congregation as a participant and not up front as the leader. This is an important dynamic for any worship leader.

Caring for one's volunteers and team members. It is important for a worship leader to invest in the spiritual lives of his worship team members by setting aside time to pray as a part of rehearsals or by asking them to share how God is at work in their lives. It is equally significant to plan fun activities with one's team members—situations where everyone can interact as friends, not just musicians. As a worship leader grows in the role of pastor and shepherd, he will likely begin to view his worship ministry more and more like a small group, striving to develop personal relationships with his support staff and volunteers.

Caring for one's congregation. A worship leader should view himself as a servant and should be sensitive to the life circumstances of the people he is leading. If a congregation is going through a difficult season—if many are unemployed or many marriages are in crisis—a worship leader should be sensitive to that. This is what makes us the body of Christ. A worship leader should not go about his own agenda, but should surrender to the needs of God's people. It is important for worship leaders to be patient and to do all things in love. This is how the worship leader can best exemplify the priestly aspects of his role. A worship leader's desire should be to see people growing in their love and adoration of the Lord. He must discern when to gently guide and when to more boldly exhort. A worship leader must build a sense of trust with the congregation.

Wise Counsel

A worship leader will often be in situations where he is asked for guidance and counsel, or where he feels the need to offer a particular word of wisdom and/or exhortation. For example, one could be on the phone with a vocalist and realize that this person has some issues that warrant pastoral counsel. Or, a worship leader may find himself needing to resolve a conflict between a band member and a sound engineer, or between two other parties in his ministry. Our staff has recently utilized some very helpful material on biblical counseling and has found them to be very effective in ministering to those around us.[3]

Administration

A large percentage of what a worship leader does on a weekly basis is related to administrative tasks: phone calls, scheduling, emails, etc. Shepherding involves managing people, mostly volunteers. Learning how to work with people who have families and "day jobs" is a challenging task. If this is not an area of strength, a worship leader will likely become frustrated and may need to seek assistance. Unfortunately, poor management skills could be very detrimental to one's profession as a worship leader—even if one has a lot of talent.

The ability to manage volunteers is a crucial part of effective ministry. I've heard stories of people who were asked to leave a given position simply because they did not have adequate administrative skills. If you do not have these skills, get help . . . or hire an assistant!

Pursuing Continuing Education

In addition to the above qualifications, it is also important and beneficial for a worship leader to attend conferences and remain up-to-date with pertinent areas of technology. These are two areas of continuing education that will keep one inspired and will help one grow and improve in one's ministry roles.

Attending Conferences

Attending worship conferences is a valuable means of being refreshed and renewed spiritually in one's ministry. It is also a means to witness things that are new—a new way of doing something or experiencing something that is innovative. When I return from a worship conference I come home with a palette of fresh ideas. Attending conferences can help a worship leader out of a rut or a sense of complacency and/or stagnancy.

Spending a few days at a conference is also a great means of bonding with other key ministry leaders in one's worshipping community: one's pastor, worship team members, or others with artistic and creative gifts. Attending a conference with others allows everyone to share the excitement of a common vision for ministry. Not to mention, with other people, attendees can "divide and conquer," gleaning more information than would be possible for one person alone.

Utilizing Technology

NOTATION SOFTWARE

Being familiar with some brand of notation software is highly valuable for modern worship leaders. Generating charts and lead sheets is one of the most accessible ways of sharing new songs, original songs, and fresh arrangements.

Currently, two of the most popular brands of notation software are *Sibelius* and *Finale*. I have spoken with many different worship leaders and everyone has their own preferences. In most cases it comes down to the brand with which one is most familiar. I use *Sibelius* and find it to be very intuitive and user friendly.[4]

DESKTOP PUBLISHING

At our church we try to be truly "multi-media" in our worship and thus utilize printed bulletins, hymnals, and a projector. I publish our bulletin each week and have found Microsoft Publisher to be an excellent resource for producing bulletins as well as other ministry-related literature such as brochures, posters, and pamphlets. A number of websites provide "royalty-free" images that can be downloaded to give one's publications an even greater aesthetic appeal.[5]

VIDEO AND PRESENTATION

Technology continues to flourish at a rapid pace. In Chapter Three I will discuss some important principles to consider in wrestling with the use of technology in worship. Today many churches make regular use of video and presentation technologies. Though one does not need to be an expert in this field, a worship leader should have a general knowledge of the various kinds of software and hardware that are available. Particularly for congregations that do not have a part-time or full-time multi-media engineer, it will more than likely be up to the worship leader to initiate the use of video and presentation technologies.

There are many different products available. I have found Fowler Productions to be very helpful in terms of hardware—offering quality products at a competitive price. There are also various kinds of software geared toward worship settings in which one is projecting song lyrics and sermon outlines. *SongShow Plus* and *MediaShout* are two popular brands of presentation software. For video, *Highway Video* and *Motion Backs* are two popular products.

I would encourage worship leaders who are unfamiliar with this kind of technology to visit some websites as a way of becoming educated on the various types of products that are available.[6]

STUDIOS AND RECORDING

With the emergence of the "Indie" music market and quality, affordable home studio equipment, the world of recording is drastically changing. Many musicians are learning how to wear the recording engineer hat and are investing in their own home studios. Particularly for the worship leader/songwriter, the revolution of computer-based recording software and "all-in-one" Digital Studio Workstations (DAWs) has made the production of independent CDs a great way to share one's music with the local community and the church at large.

Many worship leaders are now utilizing economical recording equipment to either record full-length CDs or to produce high-quality demos and/or MP3s for their worship teams. This is a great way to make the most of rehearsal time as vocalists and instrumentalists can learn a new repertoire of songs by listening to a CD or an MP3 file.

Developing the Gift and Craft of Songwriting

Not every worship leader is a songwriter. But for those who do have a level of gifting in this area, I want to encourage you in your craft and offer a few tips for your personal development and growth as a writer.[7] How do you know if you have this gift or not? The first thing I would say is that it's like having a "fire in your bones." If you feel like you *have* to write, you probably have a gift, but a gift still has to be developed into a craft. This is part of what separates the serious writer from the novice.

My personal journey as a writer has been an ever-evolving process. I had the privilege of meeting Dwight Lyles (a well-known and accomplished songwriter) at a writers' night in Nashville more than ten years ago. I was performing and Dwight came to listen to my songs and offer some critique. Naively assuming that he was going to think my songs were "hits," I was, of course, humbled (but now grateful) that he offered me some real life wisdom about songwriting. He encouraged me to make my songs "accessible" to people—not to preach, but help them respond by saying, "Yes, that's the way I feel too." He also encouraged me to read Sheila Davis' *The Craft of Lyric Writing*.[8] This is like a songwriter's bible (at least in Nashville). I also heard Dwight later say at a conference that serious songwriters know and study other great songwriters. If you don't know the names of any great songwriters you may not be taking your craft seriously enough.

You may also be thinking, "God has given me a gift. What can I learn from others, especially people who don't write spiritual songs?" God may have given you a gift, but you have to be a good steward. If he has given you the gift of songwriting, don't let pride interfere with your growth and development. Be humble and realize that as a songwriter you will always be a student, you should always be learning and growing; and, yes, there are some universal principles about songwriting that apply to country songs, pop songs, rock songs, and worship songs. Learning how to write memorable melodies and strong lyrics are keys to any successful song, whether it is meant to be heard on the airwaves or in the context of your local church. There are certain elements that distinguish a well-crafted song from a mediocre one.

Paul Baloche and Jimmy and Carol Owens recently wrote a book entitled, *God Songs*.[9] I would encourage any serious songwriters to purchase and read both this book and Sheila Davis' *The Craft of Lyric Writing*. And don't be shy about playing your songs for people who will give you honest feedback (do not consider your mother an unbiased critic!).

I would also encourage you to carry three items with you at all times: a composition notebook, a dictaphone, and a rhyming dictionary. You never know when inspiration will hit you so you must always be prepared. You don't ever want to lose either a melodic or lyrical idea. I keep a dictaphone nearby at all times. It is filled with melodic fragments. I've learned the hard way to get these ideas on tape as soon as they pop into my head. This is where the inspiration starts. Then the process of crafting those melodic and lyrical ideas begins.

Don't be discouraged if it takes months for a given song to fully develop. Be patient. Let your songs percolate. Paul Baloche compares the process of songwriting to a "greenhouse." You have to let songs sit in the sun and grow. You can't force things. I often let my wife hear my songs first. She will give me honest feedback and critique and will often suggest an alternative melodic idea that will give a song a lift.

If you are a worship leader at a given church, your corporate worship setting is like a laboratory. You should try your songs out from time to time and see how people respond to them. This is probably the best indication of a song's potential. I have quickly realized where a certain song needs further improvement by trying it out in the context of my local church.

Don't glamorize being a songwriter. If you're trying to write songs to strike a deal and become a star, you're off on the wrong track. Baloche talks about himself as a "blue-collar worker." As a songwriter he simply "shows up for work each day with his lunch box" and gets on with the humble job of serving his people by crafting words and music—ultimately giving them a means of expressing their love and hunger for God.

Finally, Andy Park talks about how "the lifestyle produces the language." Any good writer will tell you, "Write what you know." If you don't believe it, others won't believe it. Your lyrics have to flow from your heart.[10] Andy writes:

> Immersion into Christ is the fountainhead of our songs of worship. To stay on course as worship leaders, we must revisit the reasons we sing. If our song leading is really motivated and marked by our pursuit of Jesus and his purposes, we'll be singing with a right heart . . . I'll sing praises to God in hard times and good times. I'll bow in worship when he reveals himself to me afresh. If I walk the walk

of devotion to God and his purposes, I'll be able to talk the talk of worship.[11]

Since that moment with Dwight I can at least say that I am a better writer today than I was ten years ago. It has been such a satisfying journey to write what I know, in the context of community, and see others embrace my songs in the midst of corporate worship.

Making Kingdom Investments

In this section I want to highlight some key areas where worship leaders can give back and be a voice for the current and emerging generation. It is important that a worship leader has a vision that extends beyond the walls of the local church and that is larger than his personal dreams and aspirations. It is important for a worship leader to make some strategic kingdom investments, seeking to align one's own unique strengths and passions for the greater work of the gospel.

Cultivating Mentor/Apprentice Relationships

I know that many people have played a part in my own journey as a musician and worship leader. Cultivating mentor/apprentice relationships is simply a way to give back what one has been given. I made a conscious decision a few years ago to invest in one or two people a year in my church. My criteria were as follows:

- They needed to be of, at least, high school age.
- They needed to have demonstrated talent as well as a passion for music.
- They needed to demonstrate the potential for a career in music and/or worship ministry.

I am in my second year of such mentor/apprentice relationships and have been greatly rewarded by this investment. There is a priceless sense of joy and satisfaction that comes from watching others learn.

Developing Graduate-Level Education in Worship & Liturgy

The need for high-quality graduate level education in worship and liturgy cannot be overstated. My own growth as a worship leader was a fairly complicated process. I had to obtain my theological training in one setting and my musical education in another. My skills in shepherding and counseling basically came through "on the job training." I hope the path for future worship leaders will be more integrated.

The role of the worship leader has drastically changed and evolved over the past thirty years, yet, educational institutions have not fully caught up. Educational opportunities range from weeklong training events to two-year degree programs; however, not all of the necessary requirements are being met. Degree programs are not meeting both the theoretical and applied needs to adequately train emerging worship leaders for ministry.

Worship leaders, seminaries, and churches must interface. We need to have serious dialogue about the needs and requirements for the current and emerging generations of worship leaders.

Updating Our Worship Prayer Books, Liturgies, and Lectionaries

Many of our denominational prayer books, liturgies and lectionaries simply need to be updated and revised to be relevant in our current church culture. I long to see the serious creativity, theological reflection, and pastoral concern that characterized the Reformation, characterize our denominational agencies and governing bodies today. May we embrace the motto of *semper reformanda* ("ever reforming") as we minister to a changing culture. May we seek to communicate the message of the gospel in our liturgies and prayer books in a way that is innovative and relevant for the twenty-first century.

Developing a Missional Mind-Set for North America

This book would be incomplete if I did not at least touch on worship and missiology. Sadly, North America has become a mission field. Thus, there is a strong need for the current and emerging generation of worship leaders to have a "missional mind-set."

> For generations the United States and other nations in the "west" sent missionaries, armed with the Gospel of Jesus Christ, to the far reaches of the globe. But the light that was once America has dimmed, as we find ourselves in a deep state of spiritual need and hunger, searching for true meaning and significance. Particularly since 9/11, Americans are desperate for hope and direction that only the Gospel can provide.[12]

An emphasis on planting gospel-centered churches in North America will inevitably give rise to the need for gospel-centered worship leaders who can work with a church planting team to craft and contextualize indigenous, gospel-centered worship. Worship leaders may find themselves being called into the heart of strategic cities and communities across the country to cultivate gospel-centered worship.

May the words that the Lord gave the prophet Jeremiah be our church planting mission for North America:

> "Build houses and settle down; plant gardens and eat what they produce. Marry and have sons and daughters; find wives for your sons and give your daughters in marriage, so that they too may have sons and daughters. Increase in number there; do not decrease. Also, seek the peace and prosperity of the city to which I have carried you into exile. Pray to the LORD for it, because if it prospers, you too will prosper. (Jeremiah 29:4-7)

Stetzer acknowledges, "The sending nature of God has not changed. He sends us to new and emerging cultures even here in North America. We are most like Christ when we join him in the mission of reaching the unchurched by planting new churches."[13] I believe this call will become more and more accentuated in the coming years as worshipping communities begin to emerge in places where the gospel has not yet penetrated.

Notes

1. For simplicity, I will be using the term "worship leader" to encompass all of the various titles and descriptions that are utilized.
2. Some of these categories (a pleasant singing voice, musical literacy, appreciation of various styles, and a knowledge of Christian hymnody) were first articulated by Wade Williams in a document entitled "Necessary Skills for the Worship Leader in a Church Planting Situation" (unpublished).
3. Visit www.ccef.org; Paul David Tripp, *Instruments in the Redeemer's Hands* (Phillipsburg, N.J.: Presbyterian and Reformed, 2002); Paul David Tripp, *Helping Others Change* (Winston-Salem, N.C.: Punch, 2005)
4. See Appendix for websites.
5. Visit www.gettyone.com. You can search images by typing in key words or phrases. It is an invaluable website for accessing royalty-free images.
6. See Appendix for websites.
7. I have developed an instructional DVD that offers a step-by-step overview of the creative process of writing and recording worship songs. Visit www.rhythmofworship.com for more information on this resource.
8. Sheila Davis, *The Craft of Lyric Writing* (Cincinnati: Writer's Digest, 1985).
9. Paul Baloche, Jimmy and Carol Owens, *God Songs* (Lindale: Leadworship.com, 2004).
10. Andy Park, *To Know You More* (Downers Grove, Ill.: InterVarsity, 2002) 50.
11. Ibid., 51, 63.
12. From the Anglican Mission in America website (www.anglicanmissioninamerica.org)
13. Ed Stetzer, *Planting New Churches in a Postmodern Age* (Nashville: Broadman and Holman, 2003) 30.

PART 2

Discovering a Gospel-Centered Worship Theology

In the second part of this book we will explore worship from the *normative perspective*, emphasizing biblical and theological issues by focusing on how worship utilizes the artistic media of story, imagery, and expression. In Chapter Three we will focus on the *story* of the gospel as it comes to us through the ministry of the word. In Chapter Four we will look at the *images* of the gospel as they come to us through the sacraments, visual arts, and aesthetics. Finally, in Chapters Five, Six, and Seven we will explore the *expression* of the gospel as we lift our own voices through the language of song, prayer, and professions of faith. Throughout our discussion, in addition to exploring the biblical and theological nature of each perspective, we will also discuss the various liturgical considerations that are particularly relevant for today.

3

The Story of the Gospel

I HAVE LED worship for several summers at a youth conference on top of Lookout Mountain in Georgia. I will never forget one particular evening during my first summer at the conference. The speaker that year was very gifted at connecting with the students (partly because he was more "out there" in many ways than any of them). I can't recall his specific text that evening, but he was talking about the gospel and he was sharing experiences from his own life—the ways in which he had turned from God and come up empty, the ways in which God had kept relentlessly pursuing him.

At the end of his talk a line of students came up to speak with him, but there was one girl in particular that I noticed standing in the wings. She was a girl from our local church. I knew a bit of her story, and I knew that her parents had pretty much made her come to the conference. Sensing the urgency and desperation on her face, I interrupted the conversation the speaker was having with some other students and said, "Bill, have you met Amy yet?"

Amy came over and sat down next to Bill and myself. For the next hour or so she began to tell us her story. With tears streaming down her face, she shared of how she, too, had been running away from God, leading a lifestyle that had left her empty.

Through the power of the preaching and teaching of the word, God had brought Amy to the end of herself. Outwardly, she had tears of brokenness and repentance; inwardly, I had a smile a mile wide because I knew that the Lord was working in a very real and powerful way in her life. Bill's words had resonated in her heart like the strings on a guitar—revealing with perfect pitch her need for the Lord and for the gospel.

Allison and I have continued to stay in community with Amy and over the past five years have walked through the ups and downs of her life circumstances. Like all of us, Amy's life has been a mixture of redemption and rebellion. Still, Amy was touched in a significant way by the simple, yet profound words of the gospel one evening on top of Lookout Mountain. That night proved to be a real turning point in Amy's walk with the Lord. Through the mixture of word, story, and personal testimony, her eyes were opened to the beauty of the gospel in a very powerful, indeed, life-changing way.

The Power of Story

In this chapter we are going to be exploring worship from the normative perspective—the ministry of the word as it comes to us as a grand narrative that helps us make sense out of life, that resonates at a deep level with who we are, who God is, and how we are to live in light of the gospel of Christ.

In a book entitled, *The Power of Myth*, journalist Bill Moyers interviews writer Joseph Campbell sharing his thoughts on the role of myth and story. In one exchange Moyers writes:

> Myths are stories of our search through the ages for truth, for meaning, for significance. We all need to tell our story and to understand our story. We all need to understand death and to cope with death, and we all need help in our passages from birth to life and then to death. We need for life to signify, to touch the eternal, to understand the mysterious, to find out who we are.[1]

According to Anderson and Foley, "We use stories to construct meaning and communicate ourselves to another. Stories help us organize and make sense of the experiences of a life." The authors further describe how we tell stories in order "to integrate our remembered past with what we perceive to be happening in the present and what we anticipate for the future."[2]

The written word of God serves as the special revelation of God's plan of redemption; yet, the word of God is more than just a list of propositions or a set of rules. The Bible is a grand story, guided by the inspiration of the Holy Spirit and through the literary skills, personalities, and life circumstances of each individual writer.

Though the Bible is "God-breathed," God did not choose to give us his word apart from man. Rather, he chose to work in and through human skill and creativity to produce his inspired word. This theory of inspiration is usually called organic inspiration. The term "organic" serves to stress the fact that God did not employ the writers mechanically, but acted on them in an organic way, in harmony with the laws of their own inner being. He used them just as they were, with their character and temperament, their gifts and talents, their education and culture, their vocabulary, diction, and style; illumined their minds, prompted them to write, repressed the influence of sin on their literary activity, and guided them in the choice of their words and in the expression of their thoughts. Berkhof notes that organic inspiration also accounts for the individuality and artistry of the books of the Bible since "each writer naturally had his own style and put on his literary productions his own personal stamp and the stamp of the time in which he lived."[3]

God has given us richness and variety in his word. Author and theologian, Tremper Longman III, recounts how God "has let the personality of the writers flow through. Rather than handing down an antiseptic 'Manual of Religious Instruction,' He has allowed intensely personal artistry and music to flourish for our satisfaction."[4]

Unfortunately, however, many today do not read the Bible as an inspired and artistic story, but more as an encyclopedia of doctrinal propositions. Curtis and Eldredge write:

> For centuries prior to the Modern Era, the church viewed the gospel as a Romance, a cosmic drama whose themes permeated our own stories and drew together all the random scenes in a redemptive wholeness. But our rationalistic approach to life, which has dominated Western culture for hundreds of years, has stripped us of that, leaving a faith that is barely more than fact-telling. Modern evangelicalism reads like an IRS 1040 form: It's true, all the data is there, but it doesn't take your breath away.[5]

I've had the opportunity to preach a few times in the churches in which I have served. Once I shared a movie clip with my congregation in Florida during the middle of my sermon. I was sharing about how the Bible offers us a "meta-narrative" for making sense out of life. I played a bit of a trick on the congregation by showing them three minutes of the most obscure scene from the most obscure movie I could find. After showing the clip I commented, "Didn't that make our point crystal clear?" Most had a deer-in-the-headlights look on their faces.

My point was that the Bible, like a random movie clip, often appears to make no sense to us. Many simply do not "get" the story or their place in it. They do not know who the characters are. They do not understand the plot, and they simply cannot believe that something so old could possibly have any relevance for their lives today. Sadly, many do not see the Bible as a "cosmic drama" that is able to draw together all of the various scenes of our lives.

Fee and Stuart acknowledge that the Bible is not merely some divine guidebook, nor a "mine of propositions to be believed," nor commands to be obeyed. They admit that while one does receive plenty of guidance from it, and it does indeed contain plenty of true propositions and divine directives, the Bible is infinitely more than that. They describe the word of God as the "grandest narrative . . . a story told in four chapters: creation, fall, redemption, consummation."[6]

In the first two chapters of the Bible (Genesis 1-2) we see the majestic, creative hand of God speaking creation into existence. We see him creating man, male and female, as the climax of his work. We find him walking in the cool of the day with them, enjoying a personal and intimate relationship.

By the third chapter everything falls apart. Tempted by Satan man falls into the snares of pride and idolatry. Yet, here we also find the first mention of the gospel where the seed of the woman will bruise the head of the serpent (Genesis 3:15). For the remainder of the story we have the long section of "redemption." In the Old Testament we see God entering into an intimate, covenantal relationship with Abraham, then with the nation of Israel.

In the Gospel narratives of the New Testament we see God taking on flesh, entering our world, becoming one of us, and inaugurating the kingdom. Right now we live in the "already and not yet" of the kingdom. We experience its reconciling effect and power, but until Christ returns things will never be perfectly restored.

The letters of Paul and the apostles offer us a window into the early growth of the church. The book of Revelation gives us the account of the last days, offering us rich visual imagery of the consummation—when Jesus returns and we will live in the new heaven and the new earth where there will be no more mourning or crying or pain. We will see God face to face. This is the Christian meta-narrative. This is the story that brings meaning and context to everything.

In fact, the storyline that I just described is the basis for how the church has recognized the contour of the Christian year for centuries. In his book, *Planning Blended Worship*, Webber wrties:

> In Advent we wait for the coming of the Messiah; at Christmas we celebrate his birth; at Epiphany we manifest his saving power to the whole world; at Lent we prepare to die with him; during Holy Week we do die with him; on Easter we are raised with him; and at Pentecost we experience the coming of the Holy Spirit who guides us into the future. This brief summary highlights the evangelical

nature of the historical Christian calendar and its focus on the celebration of God's historical deeds of salvation.[7]

A living celebration of the Christian year should characterize our worship, regularly offering us the story of redemption as our true reference point and orientation.

"The Bible is the book of God and man," according to VanGemeren. "God speaks through the mouths of men, and men and women hear the voice of God. Though the men God spoke through lived millennia ago, the church still listens."[8]

In Scripture we find the record of the intrusion of God into human history, and throughout its pages "we find the true context for both human brokenness and human wholeness."[9] Thus, for the believer, the Bible is essential as *the* story and meta-narrative from which to make sense out of life.

The Ministry of the Word

Within the context of worship, the ministry of the word allows us to hear the story of the gospel in three ways: the public reading of the word, the preaching and teaching of the word, and personal testimony.

The Public Reading of the Word

As Christians, we find our true identity by immersing ourselves in the word. Thus, remembering the story of God's word is vital for spiritual renewal. In the book of Deuteronomy, Moses reminds the people of Israel:

> Hear, O Israel: The LORD our God, the LORD is one. Love the LORD your God with all your heart and with all your soul and with all your strength. These commandments that I give you today are to be upon your hearts. Impress them on your children. Talk about them when you sit at home and when you walk along the road, when you lie down and when you get up. Tie them as symbols on your hands and bind them on your foreheads. Write them on the doorframes of your houses and on your gates. (Deuteronomy 6:4-9)

In worship we are enacting this Deuteronomy 6 dynamic by immersing ourselves in the story of the gospel. Through the public reading of Scripture, we are reminding ourselves of our true identity in Christ. According to Saliers, the Christian assembly and the whole liturgy is meant to remember Jesus Christ. He writes:

> To worship God "in the name of Jesus Christ" is to pray to God by
> calling to mind and enacting in our worship all that has been given
> to us in his life and suffering and death and resurrected life.[10]

Indeed, worship gives people their life and their fundamental location
and orientation in the world by virtue of language and gesture addressed
to God. Worship gives expression to a story about the nature and destiny
of all things. Webber describes how the whole of the Bible is "the continual tale of God maintaining and repairing a relationship with human-
ity." According to Webber this salvation story "is proclaimed, recalled, and
enacted" every time we worship.[11]

Psalm 77 is a poignant example of the power of remembering and
recalling the salvation story:

> I cried out to God for help; I cried out to God to hear me. When I
> was in distress, I sought the Lord; at night I stretched out untiring
> hands and my soul refused to be comforted . . . I thought about
> the former days, the years of long ago; I remembered my songs in
> the night. My heart mused and my spirit inquired: "Will the Lord
> reject forever? Will he never show his favor again? Has his unfailing
> love vanished forever? Has his promise failed for all time? Has God
> forgotten to be merciful? Has he in anger withheld his compas-
> sion?" Then I thought, "To this I will appeal: the years of the right
> hand of the Most High." I will remember the deeds of the LORD;
> yes, I will remember your miracles of long ago. I will meditate on
> all your works and consider all your mighty deeds. (Psalm 77:1-2,
> 5-12)

Reflecting on this psalm Webber describes how first the psalmist was
aware of his *dislocation* in life. His life was in disarray. He was in a state of
despair and confusion. Next, as the psalmist reflected on the memory of
God's action in history and realized that God was for him, he became *relocated* in God and finally burst forth into praise.[12] Webber writes:

> The underlying conviction of Christian worship is that we are all in
> a state of dislocation. We are dislocated from God, from self, from
> neighbor, and from nature. But God has entered into our history in
> Jesus Christ to bring relocation.[13]

I know that each and every Sunday people are walking through the
doors of our church with a truckload of issues and problems; a week full
of trials and frustrations; and a daily barrage of worldly ideas, slogans, ads,
and entertainment. People regularly deal with all of this with little to no
time for relocation through prayer and bible study.

God built a day of rest and relocation into the very fabric of creation. The Sabbath rhythm did not begin with Moses, but with the first week of creation. This is why the Sabbath rhythm of corporate worship on the Lord's Day is so vital for spiritual renewal. It is also the reason why neglecting a regular practice of corporate worship so often leads us down a path of spiritual decline.

Relocation comes from recalling God's mighty acts and deeds in history—which is what the story of Scripture entails. The public reading of God's word reminds us of what God has done for us through Christ, and like the psalmist, we become relocated into a whole new mode of being. This is the restorative and corrective power of the word. It shapes us like no other literary work and like no other story. It seeks to offer us an alternative view of life, one that is far greater than we could imagine ourselves—one that leads us to praise as we recall the mighty acts and deeds of our gracious Lord and Redeemer.

Through the public reading of the word we become relocated into the mighty acts and deeds of God found in both the Old and New Testament writings, of which Christ is the central thread and theme running throughout.

The Preaching and Teaching of the Word

If God's word is the grand story of redemption, then preaching, at a fundamental level, involves the art of storytelling. In a time when so few people in Western society are familiar with the biblical story, there is an urgent need for skilled preacher/storytellers.

According to Rayburn, every minister must realize that preaching is, as it has been designated, "the finest of the fine arts," because of the significant results with which it is attended. Since this is so, every minister must determine to be a master of the art of preaching. Rayburn acknowledges that it is the most creative aspect of pastor's office in the church and at the same time the most challenging. If one has been called to preach, he has been called to be "an artist whose material is words."[14]

Mark Miller, executive pastor of NewSong church, challenges us that "We must tell God's story and tell it well."[15] When the story of God is told well "something inside our heart starts to vibrate, regardless of whether we are a Christian or not, because we were created for our hearts to vibrate with that story."[16]

Skilled preachers understand their role as artists and storytellers. Using Jonathan Edwards as an example, Keller describes the intersection of preaching, imagination, and the arts:

Edwards said that unless you use imagination, unless you take a truth and you image it—which of course is art—you don't know what it means. If you cannot visualize it, you don't have a sense of it on your heart . . . The more various forms in which truth is described, the more we understand and can then communicate truth. We can't understand truth without art. In fact, a preacher can't really express the truth he knows without at least couching it in some artistic form.[17]

Preachers must see themselves as artists "whose material is words." They must understand their fundamental role as storytellers, seeking to have people's hearts and minds "vibrate" with the story of the gospel.

Near the end of his gospel account, Luke records the story of two men on the road to Emmaus. They are discussing the events that have just recently taken place with regard to Jesus, namely, his suffering and death. Jesus begins to walk with them and rebukes them saying, "How foolish you are, and how slow of heart to believe all that the prophets have spoken! Did not the Christ have to suffer these things and then enter his glory?" Then Luke tells us, "And beginning with Moses and all the Prophets, he explained to them what was said in all the Scriptures concerning himself" (Luke 24:15-27).

Expounding the centrality of Christ in both the Old and New Testament writings is the challenge that preachers face today. Much like the men on the road to Emmaus, people today need to have their eyes opened to the story of redemption and how Christ is the central character throughout the unfolding drama.

Miller laments the current state of the church noting that

sadly, for quite some time the church has been under the assumption that everyone still gets the story. The average church leader still thinks, "What they need are facts—evidence that will compel them to change." They have bought into the old Enlightenment idea that salvation is an equation.[18]

We are long passed the time when the church could assume that people "get" the story. In fact, the pastoral concerns of the writer of Hebrews are strikingly similar to that of pastors today. After speaking about how Christ "was designated by God to be high priest in the order of Melchizedek," (Heb. 5:10) the author then states:

We have much to say about this, but it is hard to explain because you are slow to learn. In fact, though by this time you ought to be teachers, you need someone to teach you the elementary truths of

God's word all over again. You need milk, not solid food! (Heb. 5:11-12)

To be sure, the author of Hebrews is not speaking to nonbelievers, but to believers in Christ! Yet he says that they are "slow to learn" and that they need "milk, not solid food!" "In studying these verses," notes Brown, "we shall find that we are considering issues which have a strangely modern ring about them."[19]

Reflecting on this passage another commentator acknowledges how we should guard against being critical of the original recipients of this epistle, for we ourselves show the same characteristics. He writes:

> We who have heard the gospel proclaimed for numerous years—many of us since childhood—often do not demonstrate spiritual discernment. Although we have God's revelation in the Old and New Testaments, we remain slow learners.[20]

Surveys conducted by local pastors or by Christian agencies invariably reveal that church members do not know the basic principles of Scripture or, if they do know them, they are unable to apply these basic teachings.

If, through the preaching and teaching of the word, we want to speak in ways that believers will be able to understand, we must be sensitive to the methods of communicating the gospel. As a minister of the gospel, one must be acutely aware that at times he may be addressing three audiences: nonbelievers, immature believers, and mature believers; and yet, even the most mature at comprehending the word, may not be *obeying* the word and *applying* the word to their life circumstances.

The preaching and teaching of the word must educate at a fundamental level; yet bring discernment, indeed, penetrate deeply into the gospel, at still another level. The fundamentals must be learned, yet the "eyes of the heart" (Eph. 1:18) must still be opened for us to obey and to apply even the most elementary of teaching. It is for these reasons that the methods of communication must be understood and used wisely whenever the word is preached.

Personal Testimony

God's word is the story of the gospel and preaching involves the art of telling this story; however, we, ourselves, are created in God's image and, therefore, are able to communicate the word of God through the story of our own lives.

In the story of creation, Moses tells us: "God created man in his own image, in the image of God he created him" (Gen. 1:27). The psalmist captures, poetically, that we are one of God's wonderful works, thus revealing something of his character: "I praise you because I am fearfully and wonderfully made; your works are wonderful, I know that full well" (Ps. 139:14).

In his letter to the Ephesians, the apostle Paul writes that we are God's "workmanship" (Eph. 2:10). The Greek word for workmanship is the word, "poiema." In essence, we are God's "poems," the product of his artistry and craftsmanship. Because we have been made in the image of God, "the word of God is made known through each of us."[21]

Musician and author, Michael Card, notes that the Bible gives abundant examples of people's lives that were, in fact, living parables:

> Abraham offering his son to God, a parable of God offering his own Son for us. Jacob wrestling with God, a parable of the struggle we all have in finding faith. Job's suffering, a parable about the truth that God doesn't always give us answers, but he always gives us himself.[22]

The book of Hosea is a poignant example of how our lives are as "living parables." Hosea was commanded by God, "Go, take to yourself an adulterous wife and children of unfaithfulness, because the land is guilty of the vilest adultery in departing from the Lord" (Hosea 1:2). Describing Hosea and the impact his life would have had on the people of Israel, Calvin writes: "the Prophet spake . . . in order to set before their eyes a vivid representation." He adds that this was "an exhibition, in which the thing itself is not only set forth in words, but is also placed, as it were, before their eyes in a visible form.[23]

In his second letter to the Corinthians, the apostle Paul describes how the word of God is made known through the Corinthians, themselves:

> You yourselves are our letter, written on our hearts, known and read by everybody. You show that you are a letter from Christ, the result of our ministry, written not with ink but with the Spirit of the living God, not on tablets of stone but on tablets of human hearts. (2 Corinthians 3:2-3)

Paul is not interested in talking about himself, for he does not need a personal letter of recommendation. Instead, he calls attention to the Corinthians by revealing that through the grace of God they are demonstrating their relationship to Christ. God is at work in their lives, and he makes it known that they belong to Christ Jesus. Everyone "could hear Paul speak about the letter, and by observing the Corinthians they could read its message."[24]

Reflecting on these biblical examples helps us understand how the word of God is made known through each of our lives. Sharing personal testimonies in corporate worship is a powerful way to communicate the gospel. It is hard to deny the power of a changed life. Like the Corinthians, we can bring a further facet to the ministry of the word through the "letter" of our own lives—a living demonstration of the work of Christ.

Personal testimonies certainly serve in strengthening our own faith as well as the faith of our hearers. In our congregations, as part of the liturgy, we should regularly share the present stories of faith and conversion as an important facet of the ministry of the word.

Liturgical Considerations

In this section we will consider three issues related to the ministry of the word: the use of drama to support the preaching and teaching of the word; the use of multi-media technology to support the preaching and teaching of the word; and some creative ways to communicate personal testimonies.

The Use of Drama to Support the Preaching of the Word

The first liturgical consideration surrounding the ministry of the word and the story of the gospel is the use of drama. Drama has the unique ability to reveal, shock, and enlarge, thus allowing us to see things as they really are.

Drama helps us see ourselves. It suggests that life is bigger than we are. It makes space for all that it is ambiguous, thrilling, painful, and uncertain. Theater helps us know life. It gives us the chance to see our lives differently. According to Siewert, the unique function of drama is that "It says things to us that we desperately need to hear, and says them intuitively, by pointing rather than explaining."[25]

Earlier, we discussed that God often does things for "shock value" to get his people to understand his ways and/or their own shortcomings. The prophets, for example, often did things, by God's command, for shock value. Drama can be used in such a way that it is able to astonish us so that we can more clearly understand ourselves or God, or both at the same time.

In Siewert's words: "We want the people who've been coming to worship every week for eight hundred weeks to find new ways to see God."[26] Thus, we must carefully consider the nature of shock value, and ask ourselves why this phrase often carries a negative connotation. We must ask ourselves if doing things for "shock value" is, in every sense and in all cases, a bad thing. God desires that we be either hot or cold, but not lukewarm.

Drama that shocks and astonishes could be the very means to bring someone out of an apathetic and/or complacent relationship with the Lord.

Through drama we realize that we are not alone in our small stories, in the mundane of life. Rather, we can begin to see that we are part of a story far greater than we realized. Indeed, we can begin to understand the gospel, realizing that we are far more loved than we had imagined. Drama can enable us to "see" these realities.

Drama can function powerfully in the context of the liturgy to support the preaching and teaching of the word. As discussed previously, we must allow each art form, with its particular vocabularies and structures and contours (its "interior truthfulness") to go directly to God in its purest form, "uncluttered by our weak and untrusting spirits that get nervous if everything that we do does not shout John 3:16."[27]

I suggest that drama can be used powerfully and appropriately within the context of the liturgy to support the preaching of the word in the following ways: to raise tension that the preaching resolves, to raise questions that the sermon answers, and to give voice to a biblical writer/character in the first-person (e.g., Peter, Paul).

DRAMA CAN RAISE TENSION THAT THE SERMON RESOLVES

For Best, one important and appropriate use of drama in the liturgy is to raise tension, to which the preaching brings resolution. He writes:

> If we force drama too hard, we end up with unreal, falsely idealistic dialogue, mechanical changes of attitude and fairy-tale endings. Real drama takes time; it is complex, and there are no easy answers, because life itself is a mysterious interweave. I wish that liturgical drama would reflect the best secular drama and would content itself with portraying situations that often remain unresolved or in tension in the drama itself. Then let preaching take over. Let it unwind the truth carefully and clearly, allowing the Spirit to make application appropriate to each heart.[28]

I remember experiencing a particular drama at a worship conference a few years ago. The story dealt with a daughter who had come home so that her parents could meet her boyfriend. Though the two were not married they slept together at her parents' house. The setting for the drama was a conversation at the breakfast table the next morning. There was palpable tension as the parents were trying to deal with the fact that their daughter was behaving in a manner that they felt was wrong and inappropriate. They were wrestling with the tension of loving their daughter (who was now an adult), and standing up for their own values in their own home.

The drama allowed everyone to engage with a very real situation. Nothing was sugar-coated, and everyone was able to connect through a medium that was arguably more powerful than a sermon illustration. And then the stage was set for the ministry of the word to speak biblical truth into this situation.

Drama Can Raise Questions That the Sermon Answers

In Frame's experience, drama is most effective in worship when it poses a question "to which the sermon presents a scriptural answer."[29] This is another powerful means of allowing drama to function in its purest form (as Best prescribes) and support, rather than replace the preaching and teaching of the word. Questions about relationships, addictions, ambitions, love, hope, and tragedy are all fair game when it comes to drama. Nothing needs to be held back. People are searching. People are asking questions. Drama can raise these questions. The ministry and authority of the word can provide answers.

Drama Allows Us to Hear the Word from a First-Person Perspective

In some cases, drama, itself, can be the very means of communicating a sermon. Sometimes a pastor may decide that taking the "voice" of a particular biblical character—Peter, Paul, one of the prophets—would be the most effective way of communicating a certain biblical truth or passage of Scripture. Frame notes:

> Many churches today are using drama in an attempt to communicate the word of God more clearly than could be done through more traditional forms of preaching. Some Presbyterians oppose this, because there is no specific command in Scripture to use drama in this way. But . . . we have seen that specific commands are not always needed. When God gives us a general command (in this case the command to preach the word), and is silent on some aspect of its specific application, we may properly make those applications ourselves, within the general rules of Scripture.[30]

As we have seen, God often teaches people through drama. Whether we use the example of the prophets or of Jesus himself, there are situations in which God has spoken truth to his people through the dramatic media.

We, too, should think wisely and seriously about how dramatic art can be used today to support the communication the gospel.

The Use of Multi-Media Technology to Support the Preaching of the Word

In addition to drama, the use of multi-media technology can serve as another effective means of supporting the preaching and teaching of the word. In his recent book, *High-Tech Worship,* Quentin Schultze, Professor of Communication Arts and Sciences at Calvin College, opens the door to thinking wisely about the issue of presentational technologies. Schultze recognizes that in order to adapt new technologies for worship, we need to clarify what worship is as well as know how presentational technologies can be used well within worship. "Otherwise," he writes, "we might find ourselves inventing new liturgical practices that are more didactic, entertaining, or attention-getting than God-glorifying."[31] Schultze outlines four approaches to technology in worship: rejection, adoption, adaptation, and creation.[32]

The first option that churches have regarding multi-media technology is to *reject* it. Some churches simply cannot afford to purchase a multi-media system. Other congregations are concerned that presentational technologies will transform worship into entertainment. These are serious issues to consider and some congregations will find that particular technologies do not fit well with their style of worship. Because of the tradition of their congregation, some congregations may conclude that projection screens would not foster better worship.

A second option is to *adopt* technologies—to bring them directly into worship. Adoption is the most uncritical, unreflective practice of using new technologies. The problem with adopting technologies from outside of worship is that congregations often fail to consider the unintended impacts on liturgy. Adopting technologies usually ends up taking away rather than enhancing a congregation's worship experience.

Thus, the third approach to using technology in worship is to *adapt* them. This approach requires a given congregation to think carefully about the best ways to use communication technologies within worship for "distinctly liturgical purposes." According to Schultze, "Once we put the purpose of worship ahead of the use of technology, we place demands on when, how, where, and especially why we use particular technologies."[33] This approach will help to alleviate distractions and issues that end up "taking away" rather than enhancing the overall worship experience.

The fourth and final approach to using technology is to *create* it. With this approach, churches can identify and support talented people and institutions in the development of technological innovations specifically for worship. This approach encourages congregations to become more technologically proactive as celebrants of liturgical art and presentational technologies in their own cultural context. Though the Church has not demonstrated such an approach to technology, on the whole, there are a growing number of liturgical artists who are creating worthy material for worship.[34]

In light of these various approaches, I will offer a brief history of how my own church introduced presentational technology into our worship and liturgy. When I moved to Atlanta I came from a church in Florida that was accustomed to utilizing presentational technologies in worship to project song lyrics, sermon outlines and, on occasion, film clips.

East Cobb had not yet introduced such technology. Thus, my pastor encouraged me to wait a couple of years before proposing to install a multi-media system. He wisely said: "You wouldn't want to be known as 'the screen guy.'"

So, somewhat counter to my own mode of operation, I waited patiently and built a certain degree of trust with my congregation and elders before bringing a potentially divisive and controversial issue to the table.

After being at East Cobb for about two years, I created a Worship Ministry Team. Their first task was to think through the pros and cons of having a multi-media system for use in corporate worship. Though even some on the team were a little hesitant at first, everyone was on board once we talked through all of the various ways such a system could enhance our worship experience. We wrote up a proposal and I presented it to our elders at a scheduled Session meeting.

Some of the elders had reservations, but on the whole, everyone was in favor of purchasing and installing a multi-media system. I laugh every time I think of the words of one elder who spoke up during the meeting, confessing: "I'm a bit of a caveman when it comes to introducing technology in worship, but I'm willing to support this proposal for all of the various benefits that the team has acknowledged that it will bring."

I appreciated that elder honestly sharing his opinion, yet humbly desiring the overall good of the congregation and yielding to the consent of his other brothers in Christ. I had another friend inform me that she, too, was a bit hesitant about a multi-media system; yet, she felt that she could trust me.

We started out only utilizing the screen for song lyrics, bringing it up with minimal distraction midway through the service. Now my pastor regularly uses presentational technologies for sermon outlines and for photographic illustrations. We have received a number of comments from people expressing their appreciation of this medium and how it helps them engage with the message.

We have also continued to provide song lyrics in our bulletin so that people have an option. From time to time I will choose not to include song lyrics in either the bulletin or on the screen, asking people to open and sing from the hymnal. I try to be truly "multi-media" in our worship, realizing the strengths and value of various forms of expression and communication.

Acknowledging the need for a balanced view of multi-media technology Schultze writes:

> Although we sometimes overestimate the value of new technologies in worship, we had better not underestimate their potential as well. Let the technically, artistically, and liturgically gifted all join together in planning and performing liturgy. We can invest our whole being in worship—including our imaginations, curiosities, and abilities. This can be a glorious high-tech offering.[35]

Thus, it is important that those involved in planning worship give serious attention to the use of technology, neither blindly rejecting it, nor naively adopting it; but, rather, wisely adapting and creating well-crafted presentational technologies that support the communication of the gospel.

Some Creative Ways to Communicate Personal Testimonies

As we discussed earlier, hearing personal testimonies is an important dynamic in the life of a congregation. I would like to suggest three different ways that personal testimonies can be shared in the context of corporate worship. The first would be to simply have one share his or her story live and in-person before the congregation. This can turn out well if one is prepared and able to share a story with conviction and authenticity. Sometimes, however, a story that goes over great at the dinner table may not fair as well in the context of corporate worship. When it's live, there is always a risk.

A second way to share a personal testimony would be to set up an interview. This way the questions are prepared in advance and, thus, less risk is involved. Moreover, the interviewer can control the direction and mood of the interview, making everyone feel more at ease.

A third way to share a testimony would be to pre-record it. The benefit of this method is that it gives you the most control over what is said. The downside could be that you might lose some of the intimacy and authenticity of having the testimony shared live and in-person.

You may simply explore utilizing all three of the above methods and discover which one works best in your setting. Alternatively, you may decide on a case-by-case basis, depending on each individual and the best way to communicate his or her story.

NOTES

1. Bill Moyers, *The Power of Myth* (New York: Anchor, 1988) 4.
2. Herbert Anderson and Edward Foley, *Mighty Stories, Dangerous Rituals* (San Francisco: Jossey-Bass, 1998) 4–5.
3. Louis Berkhof, *Manual of Christian Doctrine* (Grand Rapids: Eerdmans, 1999) 42–43.
4. Tremper Longman III, *Reading the Bible with Heart and Mind* (Colorado Springs: NavPress, 1997) 13.
5. Brent Curtis and John Eldredge, *The Sacred Romance* (Nashville: Thomas Nelson, 1997) 45.
6. Gordon D. Fee and Douglas Stuart, *How to Read the Bible Book by Book* (Grand Rapids: Zondervan, 2002) 14.
7. Robert E. Webber, *Planning Blended Worship* (Nashville: Abingdon, 1998) 19.
8. Willem VanGemeren, *The Progress of Redemption* (Grand Rapids: Baker, 1988) 17.
9. M. Robert Mulholland, *Shaped by the Word* (Nashville: Upper Room, 1985) 42.
10. Don E. Saliers, *Worship and Spirituality* (Akron: OSL, 1996) 9.
11. Robert E. Webber, *Planning Blended Worship* (Nashville: Abingdon, 1998) 41.
12. Ibid.
13. Ibid.
14. Robert G. Rayburn, *O Come, Let Us Worship* (Grand Rapids: Baker, 1980) 213–14.
15. Mark Miller, *Experiential Storytelling* (Grand Rapids: Zondervan, 2003) 42–43.
16. Ibid., 43.
17. Tim Keller, "Glory," in *It Was Good* (Baltimore: Square Halo, 2000) 84.
18. Miller, *Storytelling*, 38.
19. Raymond Brown, *The Message of Hebrews* (Downers Grove: InterVarsity, 1982) 103.
20. Simon J. Kistemaker, *Exposition of the Epistle to the Hebrews* (Grand Rapids: Baker, 1984) 150.
21. John M. Frame, *Perspectives on the Word of God* (Eugene: Wipf and Stock, 1999) 30.
22. Michael Card, *Scribbling in the Sand* (Downers Grove: Intervarsity, 2002) 100.
23. John Calvin, *Commentary on Hosea* (Grand Rapids: Baker, 2003) 45.
24. Simon J. Kistemaker, *Exposition of the Second Epistle to the Corinthians* (Grand Rapids: Baker, 1997) 102.
25. Alison Siewert, *Drama Team Handbook* (Downers Grove: Intervarsity, 2003) 15.
26. Ibid., 16.

27. Harold M. Best, *Unceasing Worship* (Downers Grove: InterVarsity, 2003) 159.

28. Ibid.

29. John M. Frame, *Worship in Spirit and Truth* (Phillipsburg, N.J.: Presbyterian and Reformed, 1996) 94.

30. Ibid., 92–93.

31. Quentin J. Schultze, *High-Tech Worship?* (Grand Rapids: Baker, 2004) 98.

32. Ibid., 44–46.

33. Ibid.

34. Greg Davis is one such artist. He is developing some wonderful graphics for liturgical use. He also has some great insights on worship and art. Visit his website: www.writeclik. com.

35. Schultze, *High-Tech Worship?*, 103.

4

The Images of the Gospel

O VER THE past five years at East Cobb Presbyterian, as I have become more and more invested in the lives of my congregation, I have become increasingly emotional and regularly moved to tears during the sacrament of baptism. When either an adult or an infant (or both) are brought under the waters of baptism I find myself stirred at a deep level. Many things are happening at once: I am recounting the story of the family, child, or adult; I am hearing the rich and familiar language of the vows and prayers; I am watching the water with my eyes as it is being poured over the adult or the infant. The whole experience becomes something beyond mere words. It becomes a visible expression of the gospel in the context of relationship and shared community.

The Sacraments

If God's word is the story, the sacraments serve as "visible words" of the gospel. Throughout the Old Testament, God not only promised the covenant of grace in word but visually signified and sealed it through dramatic rituals: Passover and circumcision. In the new covenant these signs are now given through the sacraments of the Lord's Supper and baptism, respectively. Thus, in this chapter we will look at worship from the situational perspective—observing the imagery and experience of the gospel through the common, elemental objects of bread, wine, and water, as well as the other forms of visual imagery and aesthetics. As one author affirms:

> Words are only one aspect of worship. The shape of the room in which worship happens and the use of color, form, and symbolism within it powerfully influence the experience of worship. The taste and texture of communion bread, movement and stillness in the room, the smell of candles or evergreen branches, and the touch of hands extended in welcome shape Christian worship. Silence,

too, can be a vivid dimension of worship. Clearly, worship involves more than words.[1]

In his discussion on the sacraments Berkhof writes, "The truth addressed to the ear in the word, is symbolically addressed to the eye in the sacraments."[2] He defines a sacrament as:

> A holy ordinance instituted by Christ, in which by visible signs the grace of God in Christ, and the benefits of the covenant of grace, are represented, sealed, and applied to believers, and these, in turn, give expression to their faith and allegiance to God.[3]

The Reformers often described the sacraments as "visible words." They acknowledged that what the word presents to our hearing, the sacraments present to our eyes, and also to our other physical senses. The content is the same though the medium is different.[4]

In the sacraments we see the gospel of Jesus Christ right before our eyes. In baptism, we see and experience the water that represents the cleansing of our sin and the new life of faith in Christ. In the Lord's Supper, we taste the bread and wine, which are Christ's body and blood given as a sacrifice for our sins so that we might have forgiveness, reconciliation, and new life. The outward elements of the sacraments—the water, the bread, and the wine—are signs of God's love, grace, and desire to bring us into a deeper relationship with him.[5]

Thus, each one of the sacraments contains an *outward sign*, a material element that is "palpable to the senses." However, the sacraments also signify an *inward spiritual grace*. They visibly represent and deepen our consciousness of the spiritual blessings of the covenant, the washing away of our sins, and our participation of the life that is in Christ. As signs and seals, they are means of grace; that is, means of strengthening the inward grace that is produced in the heart by the Holy Spirit.[6]

Finally, there exists a *sacramental union* between the outward sign and the inward grace. It is this union that constitutes the essence of the sacrament. According to the Reformed view, this is not a physical or local union, as Roman Catholics and Lutherans believe, respectively; but, it is a *spiritual* union so that where the sacrament is received in faith, the grace of God accompanies it. According to this view the external sign becomes a means employed by the Holy Spirit in the communication of divine grace.[7]

The Lord's Supper

The Lord's Supper is a physical, ritual action, mandated by Jesus, through which God acts to nourish, sustain, comfort challenge, teach, and assure us. It "stirs our imaginations to perceive the work of God and the contours of the gospel more clearly."[8] Jesus used the common stuff of life—bread and wine—as means to strengthen our faith. Through the sacrament of the Lord's Supper God conveys the good news of the gospel to us through our senses—by hearing, seeing, tasting, smelling, and touching. One author notes, "When we see the elements of the Communion table, the words of the Gospel should ring in our ears."[9]

The Lord's Supper is rich in meaning and many things are symbolized and affirmed in it. The sacrament's multiple layers of meaning are conveyed in part by the different names for the celebration. "Lord's Supper" conveys that Jesus himself is the host of the supper and that we celebrate this feast in obedience to Christ. "Communion" highlights the intimate union we experience with both Christ and fellow believers. "Eucharist" (based on the Greek word for "thanksgiving") names this feast as a meal of gratitude, just as the last supper was, for Jesus and his disciples, a meal of thanksgiving.[10]

In addition to the various layers of meaning conveyed by the different names for the celebration, Grudem notes that the following are also symbolized in the sacrament: Christ's death, our participation in the benefits of Christ's death, the unity of believers, the promise of future blessings, and the strengthening of our faith in Christ.[11]

When we participate in the Lord's Supper we symbolize the death of Christ because our actions give a picture of his death for us. When the bread is broken it symbolizes the breaking of Christ's body, and when the cup is poured out it symbolizes the pouring out of Christ's blood for us. Thus, participating in the Lord's Supper is also a kind of proclamation: "For as often as you eat this bread and drink the cup, you proclaim the Lord's death until he comes" (1 Cor 11:26).[12]

Secondly, through the sacrament we are acknowledging *our participation* in the benefits of Christ's death. Jesus commanded his disciples, "Take, eat; this is my body" (Matt 26:26). As we individually reach out and take the cup for ourselves, each one of us is by that action proclaiming, "I am taking the benefits of Christ's death to myself."[13]

Thirdly, as we partake of the Lord's Supper we are demonstrating the unity of believers in Christ. In his letter to the Corinthians, the apostle Paul writes: "Because there is one bread, we who are many are one body, for we all partake of the one bread" (1 Cor 10:17).

Fourthly, in the Lord's Supper we are actually eating and drinking a foretaste of the great banquet table of the King. As believers, we come to the table as members of his eternal family. When the Lord welcomes us to this table, he assures us that he will welcome us to all the other blessings

of earth and heaven as well, and especially to the great marriage supper of the Lamb, at which a place has been reserved for each of his chosen children.[14]

Finally, when we partake of the bread and the wine we are strengthening our faith. Some may ask, "Why do I need to receive Christ and all his benefits again and again? I accepted Christ once and that's sufficient." One might further wonder, "What if a believer doesn't take the Supper on a given occasion. Is that person somehow less forgiven, less united to Christ?"

In his book, *A Better Way*, Horton compares the Lord's Supper to the preached word. He states: "One can never reach a point in the Christian life where the gospel is sufficiently understood and embraced that the preaching of God's good news is no longer required." "Faith," according to Horton, "is not just a matter of having all our facts right but of being inwardly persuaded of their truth as the Holy Spirit witnesses to his Word."[15] He continues:

> Even if we could amass sufficient information, our faith would be weak apart from God's constantly persuasive rhetoric. Precisely the same is true of the Supper . . . the Supper is often repeated because it conveys the same gospel . . . the Supper is a means of persevering grace—not because it gives us an additional ingredient or a power not present in preaching . . . but because it is a perpetual ratification of God's peace treaty with his people. Faith is created by the preached gospel and confirmed and strengthened by the sacraments. God works supernaturally through natural, created things.[16]

Grudem shares how when we take the bread and cup for ourselves, by our actions we are saying: "I need you and trust you, Lord Jesus, to forgive my sins and give life and health to my soul, for only by your broken body and shed blood can I be saved." He adds:

> In fact, as I partake in the breaking of the bread when I eat it and the pouring out of the cup when I drink from it, I proclaim again and again that *my sins* were part of the cause of Jesus' suffering and death. In this way sorrow, joy, thanksgiving, and deep love for Christ are richly intermingled in the beauty of the Lord's Supper.[17]

This realization of our participation in the suffering and death of Christ is captured in the lines of a modern hymn: "Ashamed, I hear my mocking voice call out among the scoffers. It was my sin that held him there."[18] As we partake of the Lord's Supper we are reminded of how deep the Father's love is for us. We are reminded, even as we each partake, that it was *my sin* that held him there; yet, by grace, we come.

In this way, the images of the Lord's Supper are not held at a distance. They are not framed images to be viewed from afar, nor to be experienced vicariously. We actually partake of the elements of bread and wine as our own personal and corporate experience of the gospel.

In our day, there is a "frantic search for the sacred, for a touch from God, for experience of the transcendent."[19] The Lord's Supper, through all of its imagery and mystery, offers such an encounter.

Searching for a way to explain the "opened eyes" of the men on the road to Emmaus who ate with the resurrected Jesus, one commentator writes:

> How was it that in the breaking of the bread they suddenly recognized him? Did they see the marks of the nails in his hands? Was it the manner in which he broke the bread and gave it to them that opened their eyes? Or was it the way he spoke to his Father that refreshed their memories?[20]

Luke does not give us an answer, but leaves the opening of the men's eyes a mystery. And so should we. As we partake of the elements of the Lord's Supper, we should follow the example of Calvin who wrote, "I rather experience than understand it."[21]

Baptism

Before ascending to heaven Christ gave us this command: "Therefore go and make disciples of all nations, baptizing them in the name of the Father and of the Son and of the Holy Spirit" (Matthew 28:19). Like the Lord's Supper and Passover, this institution can be connected to the old covenant practice of circumcision. In instituting circumcision, God told Abram:

> And I will establish my covenant between me and you and your descendants after you in their generations, for an everlasting covenant, to be God to you and your descendants after you . . . This is my covenant which you shall keep, between me and you and your descendants after you: Every male child among you shall be circumcised; and you shall be circumcised in the flesh of your foreskins, and it shall be a sign of the covenant between me and you . . . And the uncircumcised male child, who is not circumcised in the flesh of his foreskin, that person shall be cut off from his people; he has broken my covenant. (Genesis 17:7, 10-11, 14)

In baptism, the new covenant finds a fuller sign and seal for a fuller reality. Not only is a part of the body consecrated to God, but the whole person is baptized into Christ's death, burial, and resurrection. In his letter to the Colossians, the apostle Paul writes:

> In him (Christ) you were also circumcised with the circumcision made without hands, by putting off the body of the sins of the flesh, by the circumcision of Christ, buried with him in baptism, in which you also were raised with him through faith in the working of God, who raised him from the dead. And you, being dead in your trespasses and the uncircumcision of your flesh, he has made alive together with him, having forgiven you all trespasses, having wiped out the handwriting of requirements that was against us, which was contrary to us. And he has taken it out of the way, having nailed it to the cross. (Colossians 2:11-14)

Under the new covenant, our baptism is not a cutting away of the foreskin but being "buried with him in baptism." According to Horton, "We are wholly consecrated to God because we are baptized into the faithful Son."[22]

The Reformed view of baptism is clearly articulated in the *Heidelberg Catechism*, Question 69, which asks: "How does baptism remind you and assure you that Christ's one sacrifice on the cross is for you personally?" It answers this question by stating:

> In this way: Christ instituted this outward washing and with it gave the promise that, as surely as water washes away the dirt from the body, so certainly his blood and his Spirit washes away my soul's impurity, in other words, all my sins.[23]

This confession further describes what it means to be "washed with Christ's blood" by stating:

> To be washed with Christ's blood means that God, by grace, has forgiven my sins because of Christ's blood poured out for me in his sacrifice on the cross. To be washed with Christ's Spirit means that the Holy Spirit has renewed me and set me apart to be a member of Christ so that more and more I become dead to sin and increasingly live a holy and blameless life.[24]

The symbolic nature of baptism is at the very center of worship, signifying our turning away from false idols to serve and adore the one true God, Jesus Christ. And, like the Lord's Supper, the visual imagery of the water serves, in a sense, as a continual renewing of our faith when we witness the baptism of another and, thus, remember our own.

Visual Arts

Though God has chosen to give us the common stuff of life (bread, wine, water) and has instituted certain acts (baptism and the Lord's Supper) as signs and seals of the covenant of grace, the gospel can also expressed through the medium of visual arts.

The place of visual arts in worship has long been a source of tension and skepticism. In his book, *Visual Faith*, William Dyrness makes the following observations:

> In recent history at least, art and the Christian church have not been on good terms. In fact, when considering Protestant churches in general, while there are exceptions, it is fair to say that this tradition has had a troublesome history with the visual arts.[25]

Webber offers a similar analysis stating that

> Protestant worship began in the crucible of the Gutenberg Revolution, and historically it has always been primarily Word-driven. In the medieval era communication (and worship) was highly visual, but Protestantism rejected visual communication in favor of a more verbal approach to worship."[26]

He offers hope for the future, however, sharing that "Today, due to the new communication revolution, Protestantism is restoring the visual to worship."[27]

In our own church we continue to explore the intersection of worship and visual arts. For example, our Worship and Arts ministry commissioned a local artist to create a series of paintings that would visually capture the essence of a recent sermon series. I asked the local artist, Shawn Brasfield, to share his philosophy on the visual arts, how the visual arts enhance the corporate worship experience, and the creative process in developing the *Living Faithfully* paintings.

> ### Philosophy on the Visual Arts:
> For me the visual arts is an engaging companion to storytelling and ideas. Storytelling is one of the primary ways that we have been able to connect with others ever since God created us. When a story is told it most always is played out visually in the minds of those listening. As soon as we can "picture" it in our mind, then the story comes to life. A life not bound to space and time, but a life that is full of endless possibilities. In other words, the "pictures" give us freedom—freedom to explore and create. It makes the invisible, visible.

Using the Visual Arts
to Enhance and Complement the Worship Experience:
History shows that artists have used many forms of visual methods
to tell stories- drawing, painting, sculpture, ceramics, and textiles,
etc. It is through these forms, I believe, that we can tell God's story
in a way that makes Him visible. As an artist who is a Christian,
I feel compelled to use the talent that God has given me to show
Him through my work. It could be through the colors that I use or
the feeling you get from looking at the composition in my paintings. The visuals do not have to be literal in order to tell the story or
point you to God. The visual arts used as a component of worship
can set you free visually from the expected and open new ways to
show His glory. When we hear a story and connect it to an image, it
then can become alive in our minds. When that happens, the story
can become real through our lives. That is what God wants of each
of us—to tell His story through our lives.

Creative Process of the Living Faithfully Painting Series at ECPC:
This painting series was done in conjunction with the sermon series
"Living by Faith in an Unbelieving World" given by senior pastor
Rick Holmes of ECPC. I wanted these paintings to not necessarily
be a visual narrative from the stories taken from the Old Testament,
but rather to point the congregation to the true meaning of them.
The paintings were meant to further the dialog and connect the
individual viewer in a personal way. I want the person viewing the
paintings to relate to the color, composition, and tone in a way that
they see themselves through the images. If this can happen, I believe
that the stories become real and connected to the individual.

The meanings behind the images of the painting series are thus:
Texture/Shapes—I used heavy texture including scratching and
scraping of the paint surface to reflect the concept of struggle in
our lives. A constant battle that we engage in each day which includes our successes and failures, our hopes and disappointments.
The overlapping shapes are representative of the many aspects
of our lives and the juggling of these in our minds.

Color—The colors I used are both warm and cool, dark and
bright. These are used to reflect a mood of warmth and complacency but also of coldness and dissatisfaction. Here again, the concept
of the battle and of duality. The gold used in the paintings represent
truth and God's voice or presence in our lives. Sometimes it is clear
while at other times it seems blocked—but He is always there.

Spots—The spots represent the many attractions and distractions in our lives. The constant battle for our attention and the idea of how these can divert our focus.

Birds—The birds represent us—God's children. We are created special and beautiful in our own way. Just like birds, God has given us the ability to "sing" with our own voices and the ability to "fly". Fly through this world above the chaos and struggles that we battle with every day. But like these birds, God has created us small and fragile in this large and dangerous world. The only way we can survive in the world's hostile environment is by the protection and provision from Him who created us. Just like the birds, He will provide & care for us and give us the freedom to fly.

Shawn's works are one example of how we are seeking to celebrate the gifts within our local community as well as incorporate visual arts in worship. We want to unleash the visual artists in our church and create more opportunities for the gospel to speak to our eyes as well as to our ears.

Aesthetics

In addition to the sacraments and visual arts, the role of aesthetics is also an important topic to explore. By "aesthetics" I am referring narrowly to the use of the "space" of worship. Because a worship building (like everything else) is not neutral, the space of worship communicates something about the convictions of the people who worship there. Thus, the church has long acknowledged that what we do in worship ought to be expressed in the way we use space.[28]

When approaching the aesthetics of one's worship space, there are a number of important questions to consider: What theology is conveyed by the architecture of your worship space—the shape, volume, and proportions of your sanctuary? How do space, structure, ornament, light, and other architectural expressions help define and order the narthex, pews, choir loft, and pulpit while helping to give meaning to the worship experience?

These are great questions to help us think about and interpret the architecture of corporate and individual worship spaces. Webber offers a theological basis for the use of space noting:

> Because . . . redemption extends to the entire created order, space is a vehicle through which the Christian view of redemption may be expressed . . . This truth is expressed in the signs of redemption such as the table, the pulpit, and the baptismal font, as well as the

arrangement of space for the people, the choir, the celebrant, and others who enact the Gospel.[29]

As we saw earlier in our discussion on the prescriptions for the temple, our God loves beauty—it is extremely important to him.

One of the many facets to the Worship and Arts Ministry at our church is our Aesthetics Team. This team is charged with putting creative energy into the interior and exterior use of space at our church. This covers everything from picking out paint colors for an education building to helping brainstorm design concepts and thematic elements for a sermon series or for important seasons within the Christian year.

The members of this team have a passion for beauty and interior design, and they are growing in both their appreciation of the ecumenical signs and symbols of the Christian faith as well as the more indigenous, cultural expressions of our local church. They are a talented team of individuals who strive to bring intentionality to their design concepts, both liturgically and visually. Space is not neutral. White-washed walls communicate something. We should be intentional about everything we do in worship—including how we utilize our worship space.

Liturgical Considerations

In this section we will consider some issues related to the sacraments: balancing sacramental theology with sacramental practice; visually representing the sacraments in worship; allowing more time for the observance of the sacraments; allowing various methods of distributing the elements of the Lord's Supper; and allowing various expressions during the Lord's Supper. We will also discuss some practical suggestions on how to weave visual arts and aesthetics into the fabric of your worship ministry.

Balancing Sacramental Theology with Sacramental Practice

In his book, *The Great Worship Awakening*, Robb Redman concludes that Protestant sacramental practice is not nearly as strong as Protestant sacramental theology. He shares that there is much Protestants need to learn from others at the practical level of preparing and leading a service that includes baptism and the Lord's Supper. He describes the thoughts of those who are critical of the common Protestant practice of "distributing small crackers and thimbles of grape juice to people seated in the pews."[30]

There is much written on the theology of the sacraments; however, there appears to be less thought and creativity on how to bring out all that the sacraments symbolize (particularly the Lord's Supper). Most Protestants celebrate the Lord's Supper very soberly. As noted earlier, however, the Lord's Supper symbolizes not just Christ's death, but also the unity of believers in Christ (hence, the name "Communion") as well as thanksgiving (hence, the name "Eucharist"); yet, these expressions aren't as commonly celebrated. Here, we can learn from our Episcopal brothers and sisters. I have attended many services in the Episcopal denomination and have experienced very meaningful times at the table. Eucharistic practice in this tradition allows the space and time to move from reflection to joy and from individual to corporate participation.

Visually Representing the Sacraments in Worship

Having the visual images of the sacraments displayed helps remind us that the gospel comes to us in word and image, even if a given church does not observe the sacraments weekly. Prominently displayed, the baptismal font and the elements of the Lord's Supper serve as visible reminders to worshippers that the gospel engages not only our ears, but our eyes as well.

Though some aspects of contemporary worship over the past several decades sought to purge the church of her symbols, there appears to be a renewed desire to once again embrace the signs and symbols of our faith.

Allowing More Time for the Observance the Sacraments

Redman comments that in both mainline and evangelical churches, communion often seems "tacked on to the service, with little creative preparation and leadership."[31] Even in churches where the Lord's Supper is only celebrated monthly, the relative amount of time given to its observance is only a fraction of the overall worship service.

I have been a part of a congregation that allowed sufficient time for the elders to pray for individuals or families who came forward to receive the elements. Other traditions advocate a time of ministry with the anointing of oil and the laying on of hands for healing and empowerment.[32] Whatever a church's practice involves, it is important to be intentional about carving out sufficient time and space for the sacraments—not just ten minutes that feel "rushed" at the end of the service, but meaningful time well spent in the holy presence of the Lord.

Allowing Various Methods of Distributing the Elements of the Lord's Supper

Several different distribution methods are appropriate for the celebration of the Lord's Supper, depending on the worship space and the particular needs and expectations of a congregation. The following three patterns are the most common:

(1) Worshippers come forward to receive the bread and cup individually from a pastor, elder, or other leader.

This method is what I have experienced in Episcopal services. It emphasizes participation and involvement, and accomplishes many different things at once. First, it allows for very tangible participation in worship—one has to get out of his or her chair (or pew) and walk forward. Second, it allows one to be served and prayed for by a leader in the church and then return to his or her seat for reflection. This method also allows one to feel a very meaningful sense of community as one watches others come forward and do the same (receive, pray, etc.).

(2) Worshippers come forward to form a circle in which they pass the bread and the cup to one another.

I have experienced an African version of this method, gathered in a large circle of about five hundred, receiving the elements from the person to my left, and passing the elements to the person to my right. This was very celebratory and communal; however, it did not allow for much personal meditation.

(3) Servers distribute the bread and cup to the congregation where they are seated. Worshippers partake together at the invitation of the pastor.

This particular method is how most worshipping communities I know of observe the Lord's Supper. It emphasizes personal reflection, but is not as strong in bringing out the dynamics of community and active participation.

Allowing Various Expressions During the Lord's Supper

Once again I will acknowledge that our sacramental theology highlights many facets of the Lord's Supper: Christ's death, our participation in the benefits of his death, the unity of believers, the promise of future blessings, and the strengthening of our faith; however, only the first two facets are usually symbolized in our time at the table. I would advocate that those crafting worship consider how to appropriately celebrate the latter three facets of this sacrament; namely, the sense of community as we celebrate the unity of believers; the sense of joy surrounding the promise of future blessings; and the sense of boldness surrounding the strengthening of our faith.

Song selection is one important consideration for capturing the sense of community and joy during the sacrament of the Lord's Supper. Prayer is another facet of this sacrament that can bring out the dynamics of community, joy, and a sense of boldness about our faith.

In closing I will simply propose that the insights from other heritages within the Church are important for those crafting the time at the table and in carving out space for baptism. It is true that often the sacraments become "tacked on" to the end of a worship service without adequate time and space for divine encounter.

Webber shares that what worship renewal is experiencing is not "the old funeral approach" to the Lord's Supper, but a powerful, joyful experience of the resurrected Christ, "who is present at bread and wine to touch, to heal, and to make whole."[33]

As noted earlier, the sacraments are the "visible words" and images of the gospel. They embody the truth for us in a way that makes the gospel, not just a mental assertion, but a multi-sensory experience. Through the sacraments we are invited not only to see the gospel with our eyes, but to taste the bread, drink the wine, and feel the cool water of the gospel with the "whole of our beings."

Incorporating Visual Imagery into Worship

Because God has created us as multi-sensory beings, visual imagery can be a powerful means of communicating aspects of the gospel and the Christian meta-narrative in worship. I will offer three examples of how visual imagery can be incorporated into the dimensions of corporate worship: as background imagery for slides; as cover art for bulletins, and as works displayed in the narthex or lobby of your worship space.

I will use some examples from our own church as we have intentionally explored the intersection of gospel, art, and worship. As discussed earlier we recently commissioned a local artist to create a series of paintings that would capture our pastor's latest sermon series: "Living by Faith in an Unbelieving World." Once we began to receive Shawn's paintings we hung them in the narthex of our church. People would see them as they made their way into the sanctuary for worship. For several Sundays we had a short paragraph in the back of our bulletin with a brief biography about Shawn and a brief description of the paintings.

83

Shawn also sent me digital images of his paintings allowing me to easily incorporate them as cover art for our bulletins. In addition, I cropped a portion of one of Shawn's paintings and utilized it as the background imagery or "wallpaper" for our song lyric slides. Slowly, people were able to engage with the "Living by Faith" theme at multiple levels: as they walked through the narthex approaching the sanctuary; as they received a worship bulletin entering the sanctuary; as they sang songs and hymns seeing the images subtly behind the song lyrics; and, finally, as they heard the theme as it was read and preached from the word.

All of these ideas did not come together at once. First, our Creative Arts team explored commissioning an artist to produce some works that would capture our sermon series. Then, we began to explore other ways to incorporate the series of paintings and allow people to engage in various ways. In all of our endeavors, however, we were striving for intentionality. We weren't randomly incorporating visual images, but seeking to immerse people in our theme in both obvious and in subtle ways—realizing that not everyone would "get it," but, hopefully, many would.

Recognizing the importance of intentionality and thoughtful creativity Greg Davis shares some of his thoughts on visual imagery in worship:

> Celebrating worship through the visual arts requires much more thought than simply projecting beautiful or "cool" images up onto a screen . . . I have begun to see the power of maintaining an interpretive thread in a series of images. Weaving such a thread through a service can create a powerful range of emotion and idea that will allow the worshipper to draw meaning from the experience . . . If used effectively, all elements of the service will flow together visually, underscoring both music and spoken word.[34]

Incorporating visual imagery into worship is a powerfully creative and innovative way to weave together various themes and facets of the gospel. I would encourage any church or worship leader who wants to explore this to begin by taking small steps, seeking out the local artists in your own community and praying for the appropriate gifts and talents to emerge.

Having discussed the story and imagery of the gospel, in the next several chapters we will explore our own expression of the gospel through song, prayer, and profession of faith.

NOTES

1. Ruth C. Duck, *Finding Words for Worship* (Louisville: Westminster John Knox, 1995) viii.

2. Louis Berkhof, *Systematic Theology* (Grand Rapids: Eerdmans, 1996) 616.

3. Ibid., 617.

4. John M. Frame, *Worship in Spirit and Truth* (Phillipsurg: Presbyterian and Reformed, 1996) 96.

5. Donald K. McKim, *Presbyterian Beliefs*, (Louisville: Geneva, 2003) 98.

6. Berkhof, *Systematic Theology*, 617.

7. Ibid., 618.

8. *The Worship Sourcebook*, (Grand Rapids: CRC, 2004) 305.

9. McKim, *Presbyterian Beliefs*, 101.

10. *The Worship Sourcebook*, 306.

11. Wayne Grudem, *SystematicTheology* (Grand Rapids: Zondervan, 1994) 989–90.

12. Ibid.

13. Ibid., 990.

14 Ibid., 991.

15. Michael Horton, *A Better Way* (Grand Rapids: Baker, 2002) 119.

16. Ibid.

17. Grudem, *Systematic Theology*, 991.

18. Stuart Townend, "How Deep the Father's Love for Us" (Kingsway's Thankyou Music, 1995).

19. Horton, *A Better Way*, 121.

20. William Hendriksen, *Exposition of the Gospel According to Luke* (Grand Rapids: Baker, 1978) 1066.

21. John Calvin, *The Institutes of the Christian Religion* (Louisville: Westminster John Knox, 1960) 1403.

22. Horton, *A Better Way*, 99.

23. *Ecumencial Creeds and Reformed Confessions* (Grand Rapids: CRC, 1988) 42.

24. Ibid.

25. William A. Dyrness, *Visual Faith* (Grand Rapids: Baker Academic, 2001) 11.

26. Robert Webber, *Planning Blended Worship* (Nashville: Abingdon, 1998) 18.

27. Ibid.

28. Robert E. Webber, *Worship Old and New* (Grand Rapids: Zondervan, 1994) 137.

29. Ibid., 138.

30. Robb Redman, *The Great Worship Awakening* (San Francisco: Jossey-Bass, 2002) 80, 81, 85

31. Ibid., 84.

32. Webber, *Worship Old and New*, 249.

33. Ibid.

34. Quote from Greg's website: www.writeclik.com.

5

The Gift of Music

EVEN BEFORE I received my first real guitar, I found myself at the age of eight playing along to the J. Geils Band on a plastic, electric guitar. I imagined I was playing with my band, "Galaxy," rocking out to an energized audience. Later in high school, I found myself playing with a real band at our annual "Night of the Arts" showcase. The evening culminated with us playing such inspired classics as "La Grange," "Bad to the Bone," and "Rock 'n Roll." Most people that knew me at school as a student and an athlete were in shock as they watched me playing riffs and solos on my "Squire Strat" (that's the cheap version of a Fender Stratocaster), plunking out ZZ Top and Led Zeppelin tunes. I still have the videotape—it is very cheesy, yet very entertaining!

I went off to college and began playing more acoustically and singing my own songs in coffeehouse settings. I soon began leading songs for the Fellowship of Christian Athletes—a large campus ministry at my college at the time. Until that point in my life, I had not experienced or enjoyed the dynamic of leading the corporate singing of God's people. For me, this was much more satisfying than simply singing cover tunes or my own music for others.

The summer after I graduated school I began leading worship for a small church in my hometown. The seeds were being planted. A few years later I began leading worship on an interim basis for a young, growing church in Birmingham, Alabama. This season of my life only served to solidify my desire and calling in this area. I can remember one particular morning looking over at one my vocalists and the two of us looking joyfully stunned at how God was so apparently working in our midst. I would often look behind me at my djembé player, pounding out rhythms with his head back, his eyes closed, lost in worship. It was all so incredible.

I wrote a song a few years ago called "The Rhythm of Worship." It was inspired by my deep love for both music and the ocean. I sense something of the transcendence of God when I'm standing before the ocean. I am captivated by its beauty, its vastness, and its mystery, as well as the never ceasing rhythm of the tides. I am also often powerfully aware of God's transcendence and presence in the midst of corporate worship. Bringing all of this together, I penned these lyrics:

Standing before this ocean, this sea of so much more,
I can feel the rhythm of what I was made for.
Longing for this motion, and all I want to do,
Is yield to this rhythm and fall into you.

Lord, I'm resting and responding, I'm becoming like you.
I'm expressing and immersing my life into you;
In the rhythm of worship, in the rhythm of worship,
In the rhythm of worshipping you.

As I yield to these waters, I drift away from this shore.
As the waves crash around me and cleanse me once more.
I can feel the sun surround me, and the wind upon my face,
The current underneath me, the rhythm of your ways.

Lord, I'm resting and responding, I'm becoming like you.
I'm expressing and immersing my life into you;
In the rhythm of worship, in the rhythm of worship,
In the rhythm of worshipping you.[1]

This is how I feel when I'm leading worship through song. Nothing is as natural or as satisfying as feeling the neck of my guitar in my left hand, strumming away with my right, and singing out for the glory of God with the body of Christ. This is the "sea of so much more" for me.

Having discussed the *story* of the gospel and the *imagery* of the gospel, we will now reflect on our own *expression* of the gospel. In the next three chapters we will look at worship from the existential perspective focusing on how we lift our voices in song, prayer, and profession of faith. In this chapter we will discuss the expression of the gospel through the *gift of music*.

The Language of the Heart

One pastor shares: "When I consider the focus and function of music, I cannot do it without confessing the powerful role that music has always had in my life. I am not alone. For many of us, music is our 'heart language.' Music, whether we are gifted to perform it or not, is the highest form of 'holistic' expression."[2]

Webber believes that "Music proclaims the Scriptures in a heavenly language and provides a means through which the mystery of God in Christ is approachable."[3] Music is truly a gift of God, one's "heart language," and a powerful means of expressing the full range of human emotion. According to Luther:

> Next to the Word of God, music deserves the highest of praise. She is a mistress and governess of those human emotions which control men or more often overtake them. Whether you wish to comfort the sad, to subdue frivolity, to encourage the despairing, to humble the proud, to calm the passionate or to appease those full of hate . . . what more effective means than music could you find?[4]

In addition to expressing a variety of human emotion, Martin notes that the Christian Church was "born in song." He shares that "it is to be expected that the Christian Gospel should bring with it on the scene of history an outburst of hymnody and praise to God." He writes:

> That the Gospel of God should be attended by an upsurge of spiritual fervor and power is what we might anticipate from our understanding of the ways of God with men, and indeed from our knowledge of ourselves.[5]

Music has an important place in worship, however, not just for artistic or aesthetic reasons (though these are important considerations); or because it is such a powerful means of expression; but, ultimately, because God desires it. Psalm 98, for example, is God's command for his people—and all of creation—to praise him.

> Sing to the Lord a new song.
> Shout for joy to the Lord, all the earth,
> Burst forth into jubilant song with music;
> Make music to the Lord with the harp,
> With the harp and the sound of singing,
> With trumpets and the blast of the ram's horn—
> Shout for joy before the Lord, the King.
> Let the rivers clap their hands,
> Let the mountains sing together for joy.

As the greatest music lover in the universe, God has surrounded himself with song. In eternity past, "the morning stars sang together and all the angels shouted for joy" (Job 38:7). In eternity future, a great multitude will sing around the throne, "Hallelujah! For our Lord God Almighty reigns"

(Revelation 19:6). At the center of human history, the Son of God himself sang with the disciples in the upper room (Mark 14:26).

Music surrounds us every day. Created by God, it is present in every culture and has been a part of every era of human history. In fact, music is part of the order of nature that God declared as "very good" at creation.[6]

I love John Piper's phrase that "God is most glorified in us when we are most satisfied in him." God is glorified when we delight in making music unto him. The two are not mutually exclusive. In his article, "Music in Worship: Gateway to the Heart and Pathway to Controversy," Frame writes:

> The highest reason, then, for the importance of music in worship, is that God delights in it. We know he loves it because he commands it. He delights in the vividness and memorability with which music conveys his word. He delights when believers have that deep heart-knowledge of himself which music encourages. And he delights in the melodies, harmonies, timbres, and rhythms themselves: creations which he has made to glorify himself and to edify his people.[7]

What a wonderful, freeing concept! God has given us music as a gift to enjoy as much as he enjoys it! And he has given us this gift as a means of both bringing honor and glory to his name as well joy and edification to the body!

In addition, music witnesses to the transcendence of God and to his work of salvation. Music draws the earthly worshipper into the heavens to stand with the heavenly throng as they offer praise to God. Music also induces an attitude of worship. It elicits from deep within a person the sense of awe and mystery that accompanies a meeting with God. In this way music "releases an inner, non-rational part of our being that mere words cannot set free to utter praise."[8]

In contrast to an audience at a concert, worshipers do not find themselves present as "spectators," but rather as active participants. This is part of the power of music in worship: we don't merely listen to the voice of a performer; we lift our own voice in song. Music affirms the corporate unity of the body of Christ because it is something that the entire congregation does together. Song has the unique ability of bringing together insiders and outsiders, the prominent and marginalized people of society and culture.

In his book, *With One Voice*, author, professor, and worship leader, Reggie Kidd, describes the many voices of the "Singing Savior," Jesus. He writes:

> I think of Jesus singing with a "Bach" voice, with a "Bubba voice, and with a "Blues Brothers" voice. Bach's is Jesus' voice in the City of God—here Jesus sings with the refinement and sophistication of classical culture. Bubba's voice is his voice in the Family of God— here Jesus sings with the grittiness and simplicity of folk culture. And the Blues Brother's voice is his voice among the Friends of God—here Jesus sings with the contemporaneity and outward-boundness of popular culture.[9]

The gift of music is to be shared by all and offered by all. It has the potential to bring together all of Christ's voices and unite us as his people. To be sure, however, because it is such a powerful means of communication "when music goes wrong, everything goes wrong," comments Frame.[10] He writes:

> If in the broad sense music permeates worship, and if in the narrow sense God provides it to drive the word into our heart, something vital is lost when music goes wrong . . . This is especially true in view of the connection . . . between music and our heart-relation to God. When music distracts us rather than enhancing that relation-ship, something very central is lost.[11]

The gift of music helps us in our expression of worship; however, as we have noted, it can also become a point of controversy and distraction. While we obviously need to be careful not to manipulate people through music or allow it to cloud our focus on God, we have a responsibility to use music to the best of our ability to glorify him and to celebrate all the various experiences of life that music is able to convey in corporate worship.

Liturgical Considerations

In this next section we will turn our attention to some liturgical consider-ations, exploring some issues related to how music can be wisely used in communicating the gospel and all the various experiences of the Christian life: singing to and about God; expressing lamentation, confession, and praise; singing psalms and hymns; and writing new songs of worship.

Singing To and About God

Unfortunately, a false dichotomy between the heart and mind has long ex-isted in Christianity. In his book, *Fit Bodies Fat Minds*, author, Os Guinness writes: "Some tension between mind and heart, intellect and emotions, is a recurring theme in Christian history."[12]

This false antagonism is particularly evident in the subject of music in worship; namely, the false dichotomy between singing songs *about* God and singing songs *to* God. Some advocate music in worship for the purpose of instruction and of imparting rich theology and strong biblical truth. Others, however, describe songs *about* God as dry and lifeless; while songs *to* God inspire intimacy, awe, and wonder. Scripture advocates both.

In his book, *Worship In Spirit and Truth*, Frame notes that "Scripture plainly teaches that God's people are not only to speak, but also to sing, the truth of God."[13]

> Sing to him, sing praise to him; tell of all his wonderful acts. (1 Chronicles 16:9)

> Let the word of Christ dwell in you richly as you teach and admonish one another with all wisdom, and as you sing psalms, hymns and spiritual songs with gratitude in your hearts to God. (Colossians 3:16)

Clearly, music in worship is meant to recount and recall God's mighty acts and deeds; it is meant to teach and instruct. In Deuteronomy 32:1-43 we find the words to a song God gave Moses. He instructed Moses to share it with the Israelites:

> Moses came with Joshua son of Nun and spoke all the words of this song in the hearing of the people. When Moses finished reciting all these words to all Israel, he said to them, "Take to heart all the words I have solemnly declared to you this day, so that you may command your children to obey carefully all the words of this law. They are not just idle words for you—they are your life. (Deuteronomy 32:44-47)

Thus, songs serve as powerful means of communicating God's truth and of instructing us in his ways and his character. They are not just "idle words;" they are our life. One author proclaimed, "Show me a church's songs and I'll show you their theology."[14] Indeed, our songs help tell the story of redemption. Psalm 78, a song of Asaph, begins:

> O my people, hear my teaching;
> listen to the words of my mouth.
> I will open my mouth in parables,
> I will utter hidden things, things from of old—
> what we have heard and known,
> what our fathers have told us.
> We will not hide them from their children;

> we will tell the next generation
> the praiseworthy deeds of the Lord,
> his power, and the wonders he has done.

Clearly, songs about God are worthy of our expression in worship. However, because God desires a close and intimate relationship with us, we also sing songs directly *to* God, as a spouse would speak words of love to his beloved, or as a child would say "I love you" to a parent. Speaking to our intimate relationship with God, musician and author, Patrick Kavanaugh, writes:

> As a loving husband and wife desire to escape the busy responsibilities of life and be alone with each other, so the Lord desires time alone with us. As a child longs to have the undistracted attention of a parent—not just to play with, but to bond with—so we should long for times of uninterrupted Worship of our Lord.[15]

The following Scripture texts capture the kind of intimate relationship that the Lord desires with us:

> How great is the love the Father has lavished on us, that we should be called children of God! And that is what we are! (1 John 3:1)

> For your maker is your husband—the Lord Almighty is his name—the Holy One of Israel is your Redeemer; he is called the God of all the earth. (Isaiah 54:5)

> As a bridegroom rejoices over his bride, so will your God rejoice over you. (Isaiah 62:5)

> I will betroth you to me forever; I will betroth you in righteousness and justice, in love and compassion. I will betroth you in faithfulness, and you will acknowledge the Lord. (Hosea 2:19-20)

> The Lord your God is with you, he is mighty to save. He will take great delight in you, he will quiet you with his love, he will rejoice over you with singing. (Zephaniah 3:17)

These and many other passages speak of our relationship to God as "intimate, loving and personal." They reveal the Creator of the universe as a person—likened to a compassionate parent or an impassioned spouse—who desires to spend time alone with each one he loves. For us, "our response is . . . Worship."[16]

Lovers do not merely share things "about" one another, they often say simply: "I love you." Our songs of worship should also reflect this kind of simple, authentic expression. Frame writes: "One's hymnody is his language of worship; it is the language of his heart's conversation with God."[17]

The gospel gives us our story. We remember it by singing about God and his mighty acts and deeds. The gospel also tells us that we are sons and daughters of God, that we are his bride; thus, we sing to God as our loving Father, we sing to him as our intimate Lord.

Expressing Lamentation, Confession, and Praise

I will never forget a particular truth a worship leader friend shared with me one day. He said, "Praise leads us to repentance; confession brings us joy." At first I thought my friend had it backwards. But the more I thought about it, the more I realized the profound reality of that statement.

Just the other morning, in the midst of corporate worship, I found myself "repenting" as we were singing the lyric, "We offer all we are for the glory of you." I realized midway through the song, "Lord, I don't live out this lyric each and every day. In fact, much of the time I'm living for the glory of 'me.'"

Singing songs of praise will utterly break us if we are really aware of and engaged with the content of what we are singing. Thus, we have to acknowledge that we worship *by faith* because we can't always live out the truth of what we sing, pray, and hear. In the midst of worship we're pleading, "Lord, give me the faith to really believe and live out these lyrics." Ironically, being genuinely broken and honestly aware of our faithlessness and apathy—rather than trying to convince ourselves that we really aren't all that bad—ushers in waves of grace, which, in the end, leads us to genuine praise!

The gospel tells us that we are, on the one hand, more sinful than we could ever dare imagine; yet, on the other hand, more loved and accepted than we could ever dare hope. Embracing this truth at a deep level allows us to sing our lamentations, our confessions and our praise. Corporate worship should encompass "trumpets, ashes, and tears."[18] With trumpets we offer exuberant thanks and praise; with ashes we confess our sin honestly before God; with tears we cry over the brokenness of a fallen world.

Our worship should make room for all of these expressions. Oftentimes they may actually overlap one another—tears of lament and confession might become tears of joy and praise; empty shouts of adoration may turn to honest cries of confession and repentance. God works in mysterious ways.

93

In an article in *Worship Leader* magazine, author Sally Morgenthaler challenged contemporary songwriters, asking:

> Do we have the courage to craft a brave, new category of God-directed music—songs that don't gloss over the doubts, the cynicism, or our own humanity? Songs that refuse to minimize pain, but rather, lend voice to it?[19]

This is an important issue for the church today. Our songs need to reflect the real-life nature of the gospel. We need the freedom to express our doubts, our lamentation, our tears, and our pain; indeed, to be led to God through them like the psalmist.

On his recording project, *You Shine*, worship leader and songwriter Brian Doerksen included a new musical setting of Psalm 13. Sharing some thoughts on this psalm and the need to express our lament, he writes:

> Today, real people need a safe place to express their pain and grief, and still know they are accepted and loved by God and His people. For the broken-hearted and those who are grieving, singing only "happy songs" can leave them on the outside looking in . . . Like the Psalms, our laments can honestly express our pain and our questions, and can still have an expression of hope as well.[20]

Michael Card believes that "Apart from lament, you and I are robbed of our true identity before God . . . It is as if worship and confession are one holy fabric held together by strands of lament."[21] If our worship songs are not deep enough to express everything from lamentation to praise, we will not experience the true depth of the gospel; and our worship will seem somewhat irrelevant, unable to connect with and penetrate all of the realities of life.

Singing Psalms and Hymns

PSALMS

In his book, *How to Read the Psalms*, Tremper Longman III shares how the connection between the Psalms and intimate worship of God accounts "at least in part for the tremendous appeal which the book has for us as Christians." He notes that "While Christians have always struggled to understand and apply the Old Testament to their lives; the Psalms have found wide use in the church and in private devotions."[22] Of the Psalms, Calvin wrote:

What various and resplendent riches are contained in this treasury,
it were difficult to find words to describe . . . I have been wont to
call this book not inappropriately, *an anatomy of all parts of the soul*;
for there is not an emotion of which any one can be conscious that
is not here represented as in a mirror.[23]

Longman states that "The Psalms appeal to the whole person; they
demand a total response. The Psalms inform our intellect, arouse our emotions, direct our wills and stimulate our imaginations."[24] In his book, *Guides
to the Reformed Tradition: Worship*, author Hughes Oliphant Old writes:

Every emotion that we experience is reflected in the book of Psalms
as in a mirror. Here the Holy Spirit has revealed all the griefs, sor-
rows, fears, doubts, hopes, and confusions with which our minds
are apt to be disturbed. The Spirit has uttered these prayers in our
own utterance that we might the better grasp them.[25]

For these reasons, singing psalms is an important aspect of worship.
As noted above, we need to sing our lamentation as well as our praise. The
psalms give expression to the pain and sorrow as well as the joy and celebration of life—an "anatomy of all parts of the soul," in Calvin's words.
Ultimately, however they do not leave us in our emotions, but guide us to
the glory of God.

I have recently begun to gather some different Psalters and have started
creating lead sheet arrangements that are accessible for my worship team.
I have begun introducing more metrical psalms into the repertoire of our
worship music so that we can become more familiar with the rich language
and vocabulary of the Psalms; but, also, so that we will have a biblical and
appropriate way of expressing our doubts, our sorrow, and our lamentation
as we join our voices with that of the psalmist.

The Sunday after Hurricane Katrina ravaged the gulf coast, our congregation sang Psalm 77. We cried with the psalmist and found a way to
honestly express the sorrow and lamentation that we were all feeling; yet,
we also sang of God's steadfast love, his strong right hand, and his many
acts of faithfulness and redemption. The Psalms help us to emote in a biblical and healthy way before God in the face of tragedy and devastation.

During the period of the Reformation, there was much energy and
creativity directed towards the writing of metrical psalms. Old notes:

With the Reformation the praises of the church took a very different direction. The Reformers wanted the whole congregation to
sing the praises of the church. They wanted the people to sing in
their own language and in music simple enough for the people to

learn. This meant, quite practically speaking, the production of a wholly new church music.[26]

Old also comments on how taste in music was changing rapidly. He writes:

> The average Renaissance musician regarded the liturgical music of the late Middle Ages with disdain. Even the sophisticated Erasmus would rather hear no music in church than hear the music of the monks. This often happens to even the best of music; people simply get tired of it. Those who sing it get tired of it and those who hear it get tired of it. It was not that the music was bad as much as it was stale. The Reformation was amazingly successful in refreshing the praises of the church.[27]

In France, Calvin secured the talent of Clement Marot, a leading French lyric poet of the time, to write metrical versions of the Psalms for publication. Through the combined efforts of Marot and others such as Louis Bourgeois and Claude Goudimel, Calvin was able to publish the *Genevan Psalter*, or as it is more popularly called, the *Huguenot Psalter*. Old shares that when it was finally finished "it was a classic, providing the prototype of Reformed psalmnody for generations to come.[28] According to Old the High Church party disdained the metrical Psalms because they lacked the artistic finesse of monastic psalmnody. He shares that "With a sneer Queen Elizabeth I dismissed them as 'Geneva jigs.'"[29]

Here, the irony of our current situation concerning contemporary worship music is worth noting. Some in the Reformed tradition today sneer at contemporary worship music; yet, those writing and singing such music are simply carrying on the *spirit* of the Reformation by putting church music "in the language of the people."

HYMNS

In addition to psalms, we are also instructed to sing hymns (Eph. 5:19; Col. 3:16). Hymns are songs whose texts are not written word-for-word from the Bible—though their inspiration is often based on biblical themes and passages.

Because the apostle Paul does not give a precise definition of his terms ("psalms, hymns, and spiritual songs") in his letters to the Ephesians and to the Colossians we can only speculate as to their meaning. Nonetheless, many interpretations have been offered. In his book, *Exploring Worship*, author and worship leader, Bob Sorge, shares his definition of a hymn:

A hymn . . . is nothing more than a song of human composition. The lyrics are not copied from the Scriptures but are rather composed in the mind of the poet and then set to an enhancing tune.[30]

Throughout the history of the church, poets, lyricists, and musicians have provided a wealth of rich hymnody, crafting rich expressions of biblical truth. In his book, *Then Sings My Soul*, Morgan writes:

Hymns connect us with generations now gone. Each week millions of Christians in local settings around the world, using hymns composed by believers from every era and branch of Christendom, join voices in united bursts of praise . . . making melody in their hearts to the Lord.[31]

In my own experience I have found the hymns to be a rich source of comfort. When I was laid up for seven and a half weeks recovering from a devastating hand injury, wondering if I would ever play the guitar again, many hymn texts proved to be a healing balm. Reading the lyrics to hymns such as "It is Well with My Soul" and "How Firm a Foundation" was a powerful means of strengthening my faith and helping me through a dark time. Hymn writers are a tremendous gift to the church.

Thus, in addition to singing the Psalms, man has continued to write his own lyrical compositions from the inspiration of the word. Some of the finest examples of hymn writing come from the texts of Isaac Watts. His passion for hymn writing no doubt stemmed from his belief that the church ought to be singing from the New Testament, not just from the Old. He gave five arguments to support this view:

- A psalm properly translated for Christian singing is no longer inspired as to form and language; only its raw materials are borrowed from God's Word. In the same way other scriptural thoughts may be composed into a spiritual song.

- The very end and design of psalmnody demands songs that shall respond to the fullness of God's revelation of himself. His manifestation of his grace in Christ, and our own devotional response to it, require gospel songs.

- The Scriptures themselves, especially Ephesians 5:19, 20 and Colossians 3:16, 17, command us to sing and give thanks in the name of Christ. Why should we pray and preach in that name while we sing under the terms of the Law?

- The book of Psalms does not provide for all occasions of Christian praise, or express the full range of Christian experiences.

- The primitive gifts of the Spirit include preaching, prayer and song. Everyone agrees that ministers are to cultivate the gifts of preaching and prayer. But why should they not also seek to cultivate the capacity for composing spiritual songs along with preaching and prayer.[32]

All of these convictions concerning the writing and singing of hymns are still relevant today, and thus serve as a basis for balancing psalmnody with hymnody—whether traditional or contemporary.

My own personal philosophy, when it comes to hymnody, is to embrace both the best of the old and the best of the new. Again, when I use the word "hymn" I am not referring, narrowly, to songs found within a "hymnal." Rather, I am using the definition of Sorge (discussed earlier) that a hymn is any song whose lyrical content has not been copied from Scripture, though its content and themes are biblically-based.

Personally, as long as the music and the content are deemed worthy of liturgical use, I have no problem singing—within the same worship set—a hymn whose lyrics were penned in the twelfth century, a chorus from the 1980s, and a contemporary worship song written in the current year.

With this preface, I will briefly make reference to four broad categories of "hymnody" today: traditional hymns, re-written hymns, modern hymns, and contemporary worship music.[33]

Traditional hymns. By this term I am referring to both melodies and lyrics that one would find in a bound "hymnal"—generally speaking, songs written before 1970. Thus, I am designating late nineteenth-century hymnody as well as Reformed hymnody to this category. Among such music there is clearly much that is still worthy of liturgical use today. In my church we regularly sing hymns such as "All Hail the Power of Jesus Name," "A Mighty Fortress is Our God," "And Can it Be," "How Firm a Foundation," "Be Thou My Vision," and "The Church's One Foundation." Traditional hymns seem to be particular powerful during various seasons within the Christian year, such as Advent and Holy Week. Traditional hymnody is able to powerfully capture themes such as the birth of Christ, the cross, and the resurrection, both musically and theologically.

Re-written hymns. By re-written hymns, I am referring to the practice within the church of setting traditional hymn lyrics to new music. Though the styles of music vary, Indelible Grace, Reformed University Fellowship, Redeemer Music, and Community Worship Resources have all been involved in setting older hymn lyrics to new melodies. "And Can it Be," "Be Still My Soul," "God Be Merciful to Me," and "Jesus, I Am Resting, Resting" are a few examples of a number of re-written hymns that are being commonly sung in churches today.

In an article entitled, "What's In a Song? Turning Our Hearts," songwriter and Reformed University Fellowship leader, Kevin Twitt, describes the value of setting old hymn texts to new music. He writes:

> During my time in the ministry, I have come to appreciate the power of hymns to help us meditate upon the reality of God's grace in worship and mold us as the people of God. When my students actually begin to read the words, they can't believe that they used to regard hymns as lifeless and dull . . . Unfortunately, sometimes this rich theological poetry is connected to tunes that fail to express the emotion of the lyric to my students. The words are so rich that we have begun to write new tunes for some of them . . . Hymns take a truth from Scripture and let us sit in it for a while. They engage intellect, imagination, and emotion. The hymns are mini-meditations upon the mysteries of the Gospel that drive us to worship.[34]

The craft of setting old hymn texts to new music is impacting the current and emerging generation of believers. Young songwriters are focusing their creative energies on breathing new life into ancient (and sometimes obscure) hymn texts, finding the beautiful and paradoxical story of the gospel through the medium of music.

Modern hymns. Others, such as Stuart Townend and Keith Getty, are writing what I refer to as "modern hymns" because of the content and arrangement of this style of song. Lyrically, these new songs are rich in theology; and, musically, they are written in a more traditional "AAA" (or "stanza-like") form—in contrast to the more contemporary "verse/chorus" format. Some recent examples of such modern hymns include "How Deep the Father's Love," "In Christ Alone," and "Before the Throne of

God Above." I believe many of these modern hymns will stand the test of time, becoming classic worship songs.

Contemporary worship music. This fourth category is very broad, covering 1970s and 80s "praise choruses" as well as "verse/chorus" compositions. In his book, *The Great Worship Awakening*, Robb Redman outlines what he calls "The Big Four." These include the four biggest worship music companies that have contributed to the genre of "contemporary worship music." The Big Four include: Maranatha!, Mercy Publishing (Vineyard Music Group), Integrity Music, and EMI Christian Music (Worship Together).[35]

Matt Redman, Paul Baloche, Brian Doerksen, Darlene Zschech, and Chris Tomlin are some of the current, well-known worship leader/songwriters that belong to these various labels. They are cultivating a wealth of hymnody that is being embraced by churches across the globe. Quite profoundly, the church's hymnody is probably more accessible on a global scale than ever before. Songs such as "We Fall Down," "The Heart of Worship," "Shout to the Lord," "Come, Now is the Time to Worship," and "Open the Eyes of My Heart" are being sung all over the world. Churches in Africa and the United Kingdom are singing many of the same worship songs that are popular in the United States. We are truly experiencing an exciting time in the ecumenical history of worship music.

In addition to these major companies, there are also many independent artists and labels creating original worship music. With the advent of affordable recording technologies and the internet, the buzz to create new worship music is quite high and the amount of worship resources will only continue to rise. Though this is an exciting time for the church, the challenge for worship leaders will be to sort through the deluge of materials to find the songs that will endure.

Both psalms and hymns are important expressions in worship. As history has proved, striking a balance of both psalmnody and hymnody will be the challenge for those planning worship. Old writes:

> The church has not always through its long history kept a balance between psalmnody and hymnody. Pendulum-like the Christian devotional tradition has regularly swung from one extreme to another. For a while we seem to rely on psalms alone and then for a while "hymns of human composure" seem to monopolize our liturgical life. It is when there is a dynamic relation between the two that Christian doxology is best served.[36]

Writing New Songs of Worship

A final liturgical consideration is the writing of new songs of worship. The Bible instructs us to sing a new song unto the Lord:

> Sing to him a new song: play skillfully, and shout for joy.
> (Psalm 33:3)

> Sing to the Lord a new song; sing to the Lord, all the earth.
> (Psalm 96:1)

> Sing to the Lord a new song, for he has done marvelous things.
> (Psalm 98:1)

> Sing to the Lord a new song, his praise in the assembly of the saints.
> (Psalm 149:1)

By way of implication, if new songs are to be *sung* then new songs are to be *written*. Author and musician, Michael Card, writes:

> New songs are a major indicator that the Spirit of God is on the move, breathing, inspiring men and women to respond to his beauty for his sake as well as for the sake of the community of faith. New songs are a response to hunger, to God's desire to be praised for who he is and to the community's desire to be shown how to respond. By grace he gives us fresh material with which to worship him.[37]

In his book, *To Know You More*, author, worship leader and songwriter, Andy Park, explores the craft of songwriting. Describing this craft in the life of Martin Luther he shares that, for Luther, "music was a gift from God that had to be expressed." Luther believed that "he who believes in this salvation by Christ cannot help but . . . sing and tell about it . . . It is not so much a question of whether he can, but that he must; just as the artist *must* express his feelings in colors or tones."[38] Speaking to the influence of songwriters Park shares:

> As worship leaders, we teach . . . Through our songs, we shape culture . . . The tunes and lyrics we sing in church will also be sung in homes, cars and the marketplace. As they are sung, they weave their way into the heart.[39]

One professor has even proclaimed: "Songwriters are the secular prophets of our day."[40] Songwriting is an important craft, and we, as the church, should be encouraging our modern-day hymn writers.

In her book, *Finding Words for Worship*, Ruth Duck underscores the importance of the craft of songwriting. She articulates three reasons for writing new songs: to express the writer's devotional life, to address a topic not yet addressed in traditional hymnody, or to explore a familiar topic in a fresh way.[41]

(1) To express the writer's devotional life.

Good hymnody overflows from a living a relationship with God—when one is so full of the love of God that he has no choice but to write hymns, using well-trained gifts. Describing the hymnody of Charles Wesley, Andy Park shares:

> It is estimated that Charles Wesley wrote between six thousand and eight thousand hymns in his lifetime. His songs were a driving force to reviving the church and bringing thousands to Christ. But before this flood of hymns began, God transformed his life. His life illustrates this critical truth: songs of devotion spring from a life of devotion. Wesley's writing flowed out of his personal knowledge of God. When God is breathing upon us, we can write God-breathed songs.[42]

According to Duck, "This, then, is the first purpose for writing a hymn: to express one's faith and give others the words to express their faith."[43]

(2) To address a topic not yet addressed in current and/or traditional hymnody.

A second reason to write new hymns is to fill a need in worship not met by those currently available. Duck cites the areas of justice, confession, hope, and healing as a few topics that "rarely have been addressed but that now inspire many new hymn texts."[44] I would also add missions, the kingdom, and eschatology as examples of areas not adequately covered in traditional hymnals or in contemporary worship materials.

(3) To explore a familiar topic in a fresh way.

A third reason to write a hymn text is to sing about a familiar subject in a new way. Worship leader and songwriter, Brian Doerksen, wants to be a student all his days. He shares: "I know songs with more passion, quality, anointing, and truth are coming . . . We are creative because we were created by a loving creator . . . God invites us to be creative with him."[45] Madeleine L'Engle writes: "God is constantly creating, in us, through us, with us, and to co-create with God is our human calling."[46] Describing the euphoria of creating new songs, Card writes:

> To sing new words that have never been sung just so ever before, to play combinations of notes that have never been heard, to wonder as you're doing it whether they will have the desired effect on the listener, be it people or God—the sharing of the new song is an experience unlike any other.[47]

Through the act of "co-creating" with God and birthing original melodies and lyrics, we experience the privilege of offering the church new songs for both corporate and private expressions of worship.

As the music of the gospel, our songs offer us instruction and expression, lamentation and praise. Whether psalm or hymn, old or new, we sing about the truth of God, and we sing to the God of truth.

NOTES

1. Paxson and Allison Jeancake, *The Rhythm of Worship*, compact disc (2003).
2. Randy L. Rowland, "The Focus and Function of Worship," *Worship Leader* 8 (May/June 1999) 14.
3. Robert Webber, *Worship Old and New* (Grand Rapids: Zondervan, 1994) 195.
4. Tim Hughes, *Here I Am to Worship* (Ventura: Regal, 2004) 102.
5. Ralph P. Martin, *Worship in the Early Church* (Grand Rapids: Eerdmans, 1974) 39.
6. Lawrence C. Roff, *Let Us Sing* (Norcross: Great Commission, 1991) 19–20.
7. John M. Frame, "Music In Worship: Gateway to the Heart and Pathway to Controversy," 2.
8. Webber, *Worship Old and New*, 195.
9. Reggie M. Kidd, *With One Voice: Discovering Christ's Song in Our Worship* (Grand Rapids: Baker, 2006) 130.
10. Frame, "Music in Worship," 2.
11. Ibid.
12. Os Guinness, *Fit Bodies Fat Minds* (Grand Rapids: Baker, 1994) 28.
13. John M. Frame, *Worship in Spirit and Truth* (Phillipsburg: Presbyterian and Reformed, 1996) 111.
14. Andy Park, *To Know You More* (Downers Grove, Ill.: InterVarsity, 2002) 222.
15. Patrick Kavanaugh, *Worship: A Way of Life* (Grand Rapids: Chosen, 2001) 114–15.
16. Ibid., 116.
17. Frame, *Worship in Spirit and Truth*, 117.
18. Norma deWaal Malefyt and Howard Vanderwell, *Designing Worship Together* (Herndon: The Alban Institute, 2005) 142–43.
19. Sally Morgenthaler, "An Open Letter to Songwriters," *Worship Leader* 13 (March/April) 2004) 14.
20. Brian Doerksen, *You Shine*, compact disc (Mobile, Ala.: Integrity Media, Inc., 2002).
21. Michael Card, *A Sacred Sorrow* (Colorado Springs: NavPress, 2005) 22.

22. Tremper Longman III, *How to Read the Psalms* (Downers Grove, Ill.: InterVarsity, 1988) 12.
23. Ibid, 13.
24. Ibid.
25. Hughes Oliphant Old, *Guides to the Reformed Tradition: Worship* (Atlanta: John Knox, 1984) 52.
26. Old, *Worship*, 47.
27. Ibid., 48.
28. Ibid., 51.
29. Ibid., 53.
30. Bob Sorge, *Exploring Worship* (Canandaigua: Oasis House, 1987) 133.
31. Robert J. Morgan, *Then Sings My Soul* (Nashville: Thomas Nelson, 2003) xi.
32. All of these five points were quoted out of Roff, *Let Us Sing*, 73–74.
33. See the Appendix for a list of websites that will direct you to the various musical resources mentioned in this chapter.
34. Kevin Twit, "What's in a Song? Turning Our Hearts," Reformed University Fellowship Website, http://www.ruf.org/sounds/whats1.htm.
35. Robb Redman, *The Great Worship Awakening* (San Francisco: Jossey-Bass, 2002) 55–57.
36. Old, *Worship*, 55.
37. Michael Card, *Scribbling in the Sand* (Downers Grove, Ill.: InterVarsity, 2002) 50.
38. Park, *To Know You More*, 223–24.
39. Ibid., 221.
40. Ibid.
41. Ruth C. Duck, *Finding Words for Worship* (Louisville: Westminster John Knox, 1995) 107.
42. Park, *To Know You More*, 225.
43. Duck, 108.
44. Ibid.
45. Brian Doerksen, "Songwriting," in *Thoughts on Worship* (Anaheim: Vineyard Music Group, 1996) 87, 89.
46. Madeleine L'Engle, *Walking on Water* (Colorado Springs: Waterbrook, 1980) 88.
47. Card, *Scribbling in the Sand*, 48.

6

The Intimacy of Conversation

I<small>T'S</small> S<small>UNDAY</small> morning. Your worship team has rehearsed and you ask a member of your team to lead the invocation following the call to worship. He agrees. You take a short break and come back to begin the worship service. You sing through the first song, a song of adoration, declaring God's majesty and power as creator and sustainer of all things. After the song you read from the letter to the Colossians, recounting the role of Christ as the one who has rescued us from the dominion of darkness and brought us into the eternal light. When you finish your team member begins to pray . . .

You did not anticipate what came from his lips. Rather than an invocation, your team member begins to pray a prayer of confession . . . it feels awkward. The flow of the service up to that point was one of adoration, focusing on God's attributes. It is as though things were fast-forwarded to another part of the service without any warning . . . you assumed your team member was on the same page . . . you assumed that he knew the language of an invocation and had a sense of the flow of the service . . . but you broke the eleventh commandment, "Thou shalt not assume."

———

This scenario is based on a real encounter. It awakened me to the need to help coach those leading in corporate prayer. Prayer is such an important aspect of corporate worship, and thus, it is imperative for those leading in prayer to understand its various forms (how to pray) and experiences (what to pray). Before exploring these liturgical considerations we will first recognize the amazing privilege we have as God's children to approach the throne of grace with boldness and with confidence, enjoying an intimate and personal relationship with our heavenly Father.

Approaching God in Prayer

Song is the way we express the gospel through the gift of music; prayer is the way we express the gospel through the *intimacy of conversation*. The author of Hebrews encourages us to "approach the throne of grace with confidence, so that we may receive mercy and find grace to help us in our time of need" (Heb. 4:16). He invites us to "draw near to God with a sincere heart in full assurance of faith" (Heb. 10:22). According to one author,

> Prayer is the movement of the Holy Spirit in the human heart through which God reaches out and embraces human beings. It is a duet of love in which the action of the Spirit inspires and sustains us in the darkness of faith. It is an inward call from Christ who dwells within the depths of the human soul, and who longs to be known and loved there. It is the exciting adventure of the search for God's presence and the endless joy of rejoicing in it when it is found. It is the growing perception of the infinitely gracious, infinitely merciful Source, the Father who reveals the beauty of his face to the inner eye of the heart and the sweetness of his voice to the inner ear attuned to listen.[1]

In the Psalms we find a rich variety of expression. In Psalm 6 David writes, "I am weary with my moaning; every night I flood my bed with tears; I drench my couch with weeping" (Psalm 6:6-7). However, in Psalm 9 we read: "I will give thanks to the Lord with my whole heart; I will tell of all your wonderful deeds. I will be glad and exult in you; I will sing praise to your name, O Most High" (Psalm 9:1-2). Reflecting on this freedom of expression Mark Roberts writes:

> Whether crying out in agony, complaining with bitterness, begging for deliverance or praising with joy, the psalmists consistently accepted God's invitation to bold prayer. Whether desperate with need or bursting with thanks, they didn't hold anything back . . . Neither you nor I will quench our soul's thirst unless we decide to do one thing, and to do it without hesitation. We must drop our inhibitions when we approach God. He's even less interested in a boring relationship than we are . . . let's agree right now to plunge into a risky, exciting, expansive relationship with God. He invites us to wade right into his presence, sharing our whole selves with no holds barred.[2]

Through prayer we are invited to share intimately with the Father—both privately and corporately—all of our concerns, all of our cares, all of our burdens, all of our doubts, all of our joy, all of our pain. He wants to hear it all. He invites us to come, with no holds barred.

Throughout its history, the church has cultivated the life of prayer. From the rhythm of morning and evening prayer, to the seasonal prayer cycle of Advent, Christmas, Lent, Easter, and Ordinary Time, the church has acknowledged the ongoing dialogue with the Father that we are invited to share, both corporately and privately.

In this chapter we will focus on prayer within the context of corporate worship. We will look at the various forms of prayer as well as the various experiences of prayer, noting their role and function within the liturgy.

Liturgical Considerations

The Forms of Prayer (how to pray)

When we talk about the forms of prayer we are talking about "how to pray." There are four basic forms of prayer that are typically offered within the service of public worship: extemporaneous prayers, written prayers, studied prayers, and silent prayers. Each one serves a unique function within the liturgy.

EXTEMPORANEOUS PRAYERS

Extemporaneous or "spontaneous" prayers are simply those offered to God on the spot without any prior preparation other than one's own personal life of devotion—the prayer language that one has cultivated with God in his or her own life. Hopefully, most Christians can pray on the spot and should have something to say to their Father in heaven, in a language that flows from their heart. The power of extemporaneous prayer is that it has an authentic quality about it that can readily communicate both intimacy and passion. When a gifted, passionate follower of God prays extemporaneously from his heart to God, a powerful connection with the Father can be felt.

The downside of extemporaneous prayers, however, is that they can potentially begin to become predictable. If a leader prays extemporaneously all the time, a congregation can slowly become accustomed to one's unique prayer language—language that, at first, seems genuine and poetic, can begin to sound predictable and dull when one's metaphors and language never change. Furthermore, when it comes to prayers of confession, extemporaneous prayers sometimes lack the depth and thoughtfulness needed to capture the complexity and sinful nature of the human heart. This is why written prayers—prayed in a heartfelt way, not mechanically, are another important form of corporate prayer.

WRITTEN PRAYERS

I was raised in a tradition that never used any written prayers; thus, I was naturally skeptical when I found myself in settings where this form of prayer was offered. I have since realized their value and would like to highlight three particularly edifying aspects of written prayers.

Written prayers have the ability to communicate at a greater depth and with a broader scope than extemporaneous prayers. One of the strengths of written prayers is that they often communicate biblical themes and metaphors that extemporaneous prayers do not. This is important when it comes to prayers of intercession and confession, for example. Unfortunately, the time of intercessory prayer can often sound like the same laundry list of requests repeated week after week. Written prayers of intercession can often bring topics to mind that one would not have thought about while praying extemporaneously. Written prayers of confession can touch places within the human heart that one might not explore while praying on the spot.

Written prayers, like song, give us a corporate voice in worship. Like corporate singing, written prayers allow us to join our hearts and voices together in adoration, or confession, or other experiences of prayer. It is a powerful dynamic to collectively confess our sins before the Lord, saying to him, "We are often more concerned with our own small lives than we are with you and your Kingdom, O Lord. Forgive us, we pray."

Indeed, when Jesus taught the disciples to pray he began by saying, "*Our* Father . . . give *us* this day . . . forgive *us* our debts as *we* forgive our debtors . . . " Jesus used third person pronouns in his model prayer. We, too, should pray collectively in worship. Written prayers allow us to experience that corporate dynamic in worship.

Written prayers can be very heartfelt and Spirit-inspired. Some may think that written prayers are simply not as inspired and genuine as extemporaneous prayers. This is simply not the case. Both extemporaneous and written prayers can fall flat for various reasons. However, I think the most important factor in any form of prayer is the heart of the individual worshipper. Whether one is being led in an extemporaneous or a written prayer, the most important consideration is whether or not the individual worshipper is ready to talk to God; whether or not he or she has come with a hunger and an expectancy to talk, intimately, with the Father. Thus, when I am leading a prayer that is printed in our bulletin, I will often ask the congregation to take a few moments to read over it so that when we pray it together, corporately, it will be more meaningful. I am seeking to engage the congregation with this printed prayer. I am inviting them to pray it honestly and in a meaningful way to God.

As one of my opening illustrations, I shared how a printed prayer from *The Valley of Vision* spoke so powerfully to one woman that she resolved not to take her own life. Written prayers can be very powerful ways of opening our eyes to the beauty of the gospel. There is a third form of prayer, however, that falls somewhere between written and extemporaneous prayers, what we shall refer to as *studied* prayers.

STUDIED PRAYERS

Studied prayer is prayer that arises from premeditation. According to one author, these are "rich, deep, profound, scriptural prayers like those of Matthew Henry's *A Method of Prayer* and Isaac Watt's *A Guide to Prayer*."[3] While encouraging spontaneity, Old shares that it "needs to be balanced by careful preparation and forethought . . . Spontaneity must arise from a profound experience of prayer."[4] Those leading in prayer should take this task seriously and should be cultivating a rich personal prayer life so that when they stand before God's people, their words will have a fervent, inspired, and profound sense about them.

SILENT PRAYERS

Finally, there is a fourth form of prayer, *silent* prayers. In a world full of noise competing with the voice of God, the need for silence in corporate worship cannot be overstated. The simple act of carving out silence in worship readily has a transcendent feel about it simply because silence, itself, is so counter-cultural. Sadly, it is very foreign to our common, everyday experience, and thus, we don't really know what to do with it.

In my church, we very intentionally try to allow space for silence in worship virtually every week. Usually we offer a silent time of confession; however, silence is also very appropriate and can be very powerful during the Lord's Supper. Worship planners should give serious thought on how to carve out moments of silence for prayer and meditation within the context of corporate worship.

To a large degree, corporate worship models what private worship should be for a believer. If silent prayer is never modeled in a corporate context, people may not even think to incorporate it into their daily lives. This is a perfect opportunity for the church to offer a radical, counter-cultural response to the clamor and cacophony that fills some much of our lives. Carving out time for silence and prayer can help us to become more aware of our interior life—a landscape too often neglected and drowned out by the background noise of busyness and distraction.

The Experience of Prayer (what to pray)

In addition to the various forms of prayer, there are also different *experiences* of prayer: confession, thanksgiving, intercession, etc. As mentioned earlier, it is essential that those leading in corporate prayer understand the distinct characteristics of these various experiences of prayer. When we discussed the role of the arts we saw that "each art form has . . . its own particular kinds of language and vocabulary, and its own way of holding together in a final shape."[5] So it is with the prayer. Hughes Old writes:

> Every kind of work, every profession, every craft has its own terminology and its own technical expressions, and so it is with prayer. Those who would learn the techniques of prayer must master this terminology. There is a distinct difference between supplications, confessions, and lamentations.[6]

He further acknowledges: "The Bible contains a vast number of paradigms for prayer and a thesaurus of words to handle the unique experience of prayer. All this inspires, encourages, and feeds our experience of prayer."[7]

In this section we will take a brief look at the various experiences of prayer within the contour of corporate worship—the invocation; the prayers of confession, lamentation, intercession, illumination, thanksgiving, and consecration; communion prayers; and benedictions. I will discuss their role and function within the liturgy as well as offer an original example of each (except where noted). I have also included a number of very helpful resources for written prayers in the Appendix.

THE INVOCATION

Rayburn describes the invocation as "a prayer in which the presence and power of God are called forth in recognition of the fact that it is only as the Holy Spirit himself moves upon and in both the minister and the congregation that the desired end of the service will be realized."[8] The invocation should acknowledge that our worship is in vain if it is not Spirit-inspired. Often, the invocation will also employ the language of adoration and praise, which is very fitting in light of the vertical, God-focused dimension of this prayer.

A Prayer of Invocation:

Almighty God,
we praise you for your glorious majesty,
and we acknowledge that without you our worship is in vain.
Come, inhabit our praise:
fill us with a sense of expectancy,
enliven our songs,
inspire our prayers,
illuminate your word.
May we know your presence in this place.
Through Christ, our Lord. Amen.

THE PRAYER OF CONFESSION

Frame states that "When we approach God in prayer, we should approach him not only as servants, but also as sinners saved by grace . . . Although God forgives our sins once for all in Christ, we may not forget about sin as we approach God's presence."[9] The prayer of confession is a beautiful picture of the gospel: that we are more sinful that we could ever dare imagine, but more loved and forgiven than we could ever dare hope. In a culture that avoids talk of sin, regular prayers of confession foster honesty and openness in our relationship with God. Just as a marriage cannot flourish without honest confession, so our marriage-like relationship with God cannot flourish unless we freely and honestly express all facets of our life: hopes, fears, sins, desires, thanksgiving, and praise.[10]

The confession of sin and assurance of pardon is often the most explicitly dialogic aspect of a worship service, alternating between our words to God and God's word to us. The prayer of confession invites us to speak words that are unreservedly honest about our own sin, words that often do not come naturally in our relationship with God or with our fellow human beings. Such honesty becomes profoundly liberating in the context of God's grace.

A Prayer of Confession:

Holy God,
We acknowledge the depth of our sin to you:
we confess that we are too often wrapped up in our own small lives:
too often enamored with ourselves, than captivated by you;
too often worried about our own agendas, than resting in your
    goodness;
too often trying to make a name for ourselves, than honoring
    yours;
too often boasting in our strengths, than bowing in brokenness
    before you.
Give us an undivided heart; be our greatest desire.
Forgive us for all the ways we fall short,
all the ways we fail to believe the gospel.
Through Christ, our Lord. Amen.

THE PRAYER OF LAMENT

Prayers of lament are an "implicit act of faith in which the community of faith turns to God as its only source of hope and comfort."[11] Just as we discussed the need for more songs of lament in the previous chapter, we need to cultivate *prayers* of lament in our worship as well. Prayers of lament can serve well as extensions of the prayer of confession—as we confess our sin, we lament that God's kingdom has not yet fully come. One of the best ways to begin cultivating the language of lament is through the Psalms.

A Prayer of Lament:

> How long, O Lord? Will your forget me forever? How long will you hide your face from me? How long must I wrestle with my thoughts and every day have sorrow in my heart? How long will my enemy triumph over me? Look on me and answer, O Lord my God. Give light to my eyes, or I will sleep in death; My enemy will say, "I have overcome him," and my foes will rejoice when I fall. But I trust in your unfailing love; my heart rejoices in your salvation. I will sing to the Lord, for he has been good to me. (Psalm 13)

SCRIPTURAL ASSURANCES OF GOD'S FORGIVING GRACE

During a seminary lecture several years ago, Marva Dawn—a respected voice in worship—made the comment: "You cannot have the confession without the absolution." In other words, the absolution, or the word of assurance of God's forgiving grace, is what allows us to be completely transparent and boldly honest about our condition. Without the context of grace, we would be miserably despairing in our confessions.

Scriptural Assurances of Pardon:

> The Lord is merciful and gracious, slow to anger and abounding in steadfast love. He does not deal with us according to our sins, nor requite us according to our iniquities. For as the heavens are high above the earth, so great is his steadfast love toward those who fear him; as far as the east is from the west, so far does he remove our transgressions from us. (Psalm 103:8, 10-12)

> If we say we have no sin, we deceive ourselves, and the truth is not in us. If we confess our sins, he is faithful and just, and will forgive our sins and cleanse us from all unrighteousness. (1 John 1:8-9; 2:1-2)

> He himself bore our sins in his body on the cross, so that, free from sins, we might live for righteousness; by his wounds you have been healed. (1 Peter 2:24)

THE PRAYER OF INTERCESSION

Through intercessory prayer we address God in a special way as priestly intercessors for each other and for the world at large. We pray not just for our own congregation and for the people we know; we also intercede for those in authority, for those suffering oppression, for those who are poor, hungry, and sick.

According to Old, one of the reasons that we come together in assemblies of worship is to pray for the coming of the kingdom, for the progress of the gospel, the reforming of society, and the building up of the Church. He adds that "One of the distinctions between public prayer and private prayer is that in public prayer we pray as a community, for the community, and for the concerns of the community."[12]

A friend wrote the following prayer. He is one of the pastors of a new church plant in Berkeley, California. His prayer reveals both a heart for and awareness of a world with needs larger than his own.

A Prayer of Intercession:

> O Lord, even as we sing your praises, and apprehend your beauty, and reflect upon your goodness and wisdom, we remember that we live in a fractured world—one that is ridden with self-destructive agendas and self-exalting motivations. We pray for our world, that you would bring resolution and peace where there is conflict and strife, particularly in Iraq and Israel. We pray for our city, that you would bring help to the poor and mercy to the weak. We pray that in all places your justice would roll down like a river over all tyranny, evil, and inequity. We pray that you would change us and move us from self-security to self-sacrifice. Bind us together with all peoples and with your creation and with yourself in equity, fulfillment, and delight. These things we ask in Christ's name. Amen. (Jonathan St. Clair, Pastor of Spiritual Formation, Christ Church of Berkeley, 2006)

THE PRAYER OF ILLUMINATION

Old states that "the fundamental concern of the Prayer of Illumination is to pray that through the inner working of the Holy Spirit, the reading and preaching of the Scriptures might be heard with true understanding and might bear fruit in the enlightening and building up of the congregation."[13] Indeed, this prayer captures the heart of this book! We need our eyes opened to the beauty and paradox of the gospel. Because we suffer from spiritual blindness, we need to ask the Holy Spirit to help us see, hear, and experience all of the promises of the gospel.

A Prayer of Illumination:

Lord God,
give us a spirit of wisdom and of revelation in the knowledge
   of Christ,
so that the eyes of our hearts might be enlightened.
Help us to know the hope to which you have called us,
the riches of the glorious inheritance in the saints,
and the immeasurable greatness of your power at work in us.
Through Christ, our Lord. Amen. (based on Ephesians 1:17-19)

THE PRAYER OF THANKSGIVING

James tells us that "Every good and perfect gift comes from God in heaven" (James 1:16). Thus, "To God we owe everything that we are and everything that we have."[14] We also claim the promise that God "works all things for the good of those who love him, who have been called according to his purpose" (Romans 8:28). Therefore, biblical prayer abounds in thanks for all the various circumstances of life. Frame shares that "God's people rejoice even in suffering, as did the apostles after they had been flogged, 'because they had been counted worthy of suffering disgrace for the Name' (Acts 5:41)." We do not give thanks for sickness, pain, Satan, and sin. But we thank God for his good purposes in allowing these into our lives—good purposes that will in his time lead to the end of all our sin and suffering.[15]

I have found that most people blend prayers of praise and adoration with prayers of thanksgiving. There is a difference, however. Prayers of praise and adoration emphasize *who God is*; prayers of thanksgiving emphasize *what God has done*. Old writes:

> Praise comes out of the experience of awe that wells up within us when we are confronted by God's presence . . . Thanksgiving, on the other hand, is a recognition that God has blessed us . . . Thanksgiving is a recognition of the obligation we have to God because he has blessed us. It is a witness to the world that God has helped us in time of need and a confession of the responsibility which that puts on us.[16]

Making the distinction between praise and thanksgiving will allow the uniqueness of each to focus and enhance our experience of prayer.

A member of my congregation wrote the following prayer, and we recently used it in a Good Friday service. I'm sure this prayer was written out of the overflow of personal experience, yet its language touches all of us, making it broadly accessible. This is part of the art and craft of songwriting—turning something personal into something universal. It is also part of the art and craft of writing prayers for liturgical use. I long to see more and more of the rich poetry and theology of written prayers celebrated and unleashed within the church at large as well as within our own local community.

A Prayer of Thanksgiving:

> Dearest Lord Jesus, I thank you that you understand my pain.
> You who were immortal took on flesh that is fragile.
> You, though innocent, were falsely accused.

You, utterly perfect, went undefended at trial.
You were stripped naked, humiliated to cover my shame.
You endured the beating my sins deserved.
You exhausted your strength when you carried my cross.
Your hands, which never did evil, were nailed to the wood.
Your feet, which never strayed from the right path,
were pierced to bring me good news.
You, who gave life—
you, the very Word of life—
faced the curse of death in my place.
You, who never disappointed your Father,
bore his fury for my sake.
You, who conquered death,
who sit at the right hand of Almighty God,
are at this moment interceding with him on my behalf.
Thank you, my sweet Savior,
that my suffering is as nothing in comparison
to your goodness to me. (Marie Beard, 2006)

THE PRAYER OF CONSECRATION

Prayers of consecration are very appropriate in the context of corporate worship. Particularly after a message, a prayer of consecration is a fitting response to the ministry of the word. Often a prayer of consecration can be followed by a psalm or hymn that captures that theme as well. Singing the modern hymn "In Christ Alone," for example, is a powerful way to respond to this prayer of St. Patrick.

A Prayer of Consecration:

I bind unto myself today
the power of God to hold and lead,
his eye to watch, his might to stay,
his ear to hearken to my need:
the wisdom of my God to teach,
his hand to guide, his shield to ward;
the word of God to give me speech,
his heavenly host to be my guard.

Christ be with me, Christ before me,
Christ behind me, Christ deep within me,
Christ below me, Christ above me,
Christ at my right hand, Christ at my left hand,
Christ as I lie down, Christ as I arise,

Christ as I stand,
Christ in the heart of everyone who thinks of me,
Christ in the mouth of everyone who speaks to me,
Christ in every eye that sees me,
Christ in every ear that hears me. (from St. Patrick's breastplate) [17]

COMMUNION PRAYERS

Traditionally, three prayers are offered throughout the sacrament of communion: first, the communion invocation at the beginning of the celebration of the sacrament; second, the prayer of thanksgiving (Eucharistic prayer) over the bread and wine; and third, a prayer after communion that gives thanks for the grace received in the sacrament and as a consequence promises the dedication of ourselves to God's service. [18]

A Communion Invocation:

Heavenly Father, we worship you as the Maker of all things visible and invisible. We thank you for the tangible expressions of the gospel revealed in the common elements of bread and wine. As we come to this table spread before us—instituted in time, experienced in the present, fulfilled in your return—we come laying our burdens before you, seeking grace and sustenance in our journey of faith. We pray for the Church and ask that you would strengthen, protect, and purify her, that she might be a witness to the world, and an instrument in your hand; through Christ our Lord. Amen.

A Prayer of Thanksgiving (Eucharistic Prayer):

Holy, holy, holy is the Lord God Almighty, who was, and is, and is to come. With thankful hearts we come acknowledging and recounting your mighty acts and deeds. Like the psalmist, we desire to relocate ourselves in the story of salvation, a story of which we are a part. We remember the way you chose a nation and a people and made them your own. Even though they often turned their back on you, in your mercy you always forgave them. Even though they were often unfaithful, you loved them with a steadfast love. In time and history you proved your love, not only to one nation, but to all peoples by sending your one and only Son as the final sacrifice and atonement for sin. You sent your Holy Spirit to sanctify and to bless us; and we wait, expectantly, for your return, for the final Wedding Feast of the

117

Lamb. Until that day, we turn our hearts and minds to these elements before us: the bread, a symbol of your body that was broken for us; the wine, a symbol of your blood that was poured out for us. We find, here, our source of strength in the grace of the gospel, revealed in this meal, of which we now partake—members of one body, believers of one name, Jesus Christ, our Lord. Amen.

A Prayer after Communion:

Triune God, we thank you that through this meal you have visually and experientially demonstrated your goodness and love toward us. We would ask that you would fill us with your grace to live more and more for you and for your glory. We would strive to serve you and love you with an undivided heart each and every day; through Jesus Christ, our Lord, who lives and reigns, and who, through the Father and the Holy Spirit, is worshipped and glorified. Amen.

The Benediction

I remember when the true beauty and significance of the Benediction struck me for the first time. I used to think of the Benediction as just a closing rubric of worship. Then, one day, I realized that this was God's prayer over me, over us as a congregation. This was his grace as a closing expression before the people are dismissed and sent out to be a witnesses and pilgrims in the world. "Just as we begin with God's gracious invitation, so we end with God's promise to always be with us."[19]

Scriptural Examples of a Benediction:

The Lord bless you and keep you;
the Lord make his face to shine upon you and be gracious to you;
the Lord turn his face toward you and give you peace. (Numbers 6:24-26)

———

The grace of the Lord Jesus Christ,
the love of God,
and the communion of the Holy Spirit
be with all of you. (2 Corinthians 13:13)

———

> Peace I leave with you;
> my peace I give to you;
> not as the world gives do I give to you.
> Let not your hearts be troubled,
> neither let them be afraid. (John 14:27)

Prayer allows us to interact with God in a gospel-dialogue. To be able to come to the throne of grace privately and corporately in worship is an amazing privilege. For those crafting liturgies, we would serve our people well by incorporating all of the various forms and experiences of prayer in our worship gatherings.

NOTES

1. Excerpt from *The Glenstal Book of Prayer* (Collegeville, Minn.: Liturgical, 2001) 11.
2. Mark Roberts, *No Holds Barred* (Colorado Springs: Waterbrook, 2005) 7.
3. Terry Johnson, *Leading in Worship* (Oak Ridge, Tenn.: Covenant Foundation, 1996) 16.
4. Hughes Oliphant Old, *Leading in Prayer* (Grand Rapids: Eerdmans, 1995) 5.
5. Harold M. Best, *Unceasing Worship* (Downers Grove, Ill.: InterVarsity, 2003) 157.
6. Old, *Leading in Prayer*, 7.
7. Ibid.
8. Robert G. Rayburn, *O Come, Let us Worship* (Grand Rapids: Baker, 1980) 180.
9. John M. Frame, *Worship in Spirit and Truth* (Phillipsburg, N.J.: Presbyterian and Reformed, 1996) 103.
10. *The Worship Sourcebook* (Grand Rapids: CRC, 2004) 81.
11. Ibid., 111.
12. Old, *Leading in Prayer*, 175.
13. Ibid., 144.
14. Frame, *Worship in Spirit and Truth*, 103.
15. Ibid., 104.
16. Old, *Leading in Prayer*, 291.
17. Excerpt from *The Glenstal Book of Prayer* (Collegeville: Liturgical, 2001) 96.
18. Old, *Leading in Prayer*, 225.
19. *The Worship Sourcebook*, 360.

7

The Heritage of Truth

IN OUR North American culture, it is hard for us to imagine having to die for our faith, but that has been the harsh reality for much of the church throughout the ages. During the time of the Reformation, for example, members of Reformed churches in the Netherlands stood courageously against the threat of persecution and death. Rather than deny what they believed to be true, petitioners of the *Belgic Confession* were prepared to "offer their backs to stripes, their tongues to knives, their mouths to gags, and their whole bodies to the fire, well knowing that those who follow Christ must take His cross and deny themselves."[1]

Professing Our Faith

It is easy for us to forget the climate in which so many of our confessions of faith were written; yet the words we proclaim together in our corporate worship settings were, at one point in time, a matter of life or death.

In this chapter we will continue to look at worship from the existential perspective, now highlighting our expression of the gospel through the *heritage of truth*. In a culture that triumphs individualism, professions of faith underscore the corporate nature of the church, bringing a sense of unity and heritage to our worship experience. The following introductions to the profession of faith call attention to the various purposes for the corporate recitation of a scriptural or historic creed:[2]

Let us together profess our faith . . .

Let us affirm our faith . . .

Let us join with all the saints in all cultures and ages in our profession of faith and praise . . .

Let us together confess the faith of the church at all times and in all places . . .

Let us express our unity with the church of all ages by professing our faith in the words . . .

Frame states that a creed "is simply the church's statement of what it believes the Scriptures to teach." He shares that "When people meet in the name of Christ, it is altogether fitting that they identify themselves as His people. A creed does that, by setting forth the gospel."[3] Rayburn writes, "How thankful believers should be that in ages past faithful men fought for the truth and preserved the truth of the Scriptures in their creedal statements."[4]

Creeds have usually emerged during major turning points in the history of the church; particularly during four critical periods when it was necessary for the church to differentiate itself from others in the environment. The first such turning point was Israel's division from the nations in her exodus from Egypt. Moses defined Israel's monotheistic faith in the *shema* of Deuteronomy 6 ("Hear, O Israel: The Lord our God is one Lord").[5]

The second turning point came with Christ. Writers of the New Testament wanted to distinguish the infant church's understanding of Christ from the views of its Jewish mother, and they often incorporated short summaries of that faith in their writings (e.g. Colossians 1:15-20).[6]

The third turning point came during the early growth of the church. The ecumenical creeds (e.g., The Apostles' Creed) represent the ways in which the ancient church defined its faith in a Gentile world rich in competing philosophies and religions (e.g., Platonism and Gnosticism).[7]

The fourth turning point came during the Protestant Reformation. The sixteenth and seventeenth century Reformed churches produced several families of orthodox Reformed confessions that differentiated the Reformed faith from both Roman Catholicism and other Protestant churches.

Liturgical Considerations

In this section we will explore some common examples of professions of faith, highlighting their historical background and liturgical use. In addition to ecumenical creeds (Apostles' Creed, Nicene Creed), I will also draw attention to two confessions (Belgic Confession, Westminster Confession of Faith) and three catechisms (Heidelberg Catechism, Westminster Shorter and Larger Catechisms). Though other historic and theologically significant confessions and catechisms exist, I am narrowing the discussion to these five because, in my experience, they tend to be the most appropriate for *liturgical* use.

Creeds

THE APOSTLES' CREED

This creed is called *The Apostles' Creed* not because it was produced by the apostles themselves but because it contains a brief summary of their teachings. It sets forth their doctrine "in sublime simplicity, in unsurpassable brevity, in beautiful order, and with liturgical solemnity."[8] In its present form it is dated no later than the fourth century. The ancient church used this creed to identify believers, to instruct new converts, and to provide a unifying confession of faith for worship and liturgy.[9]

> I believe in God, the Father almighty,
>> Maker of heaven and earth.
>
> I believe in Jesus Christ, his only Son, our Lord,
>> who was conceived by the Holy Spirit,
>> and born of the virgin Mary.
>> He suffered under Pontius Pilate,
>> was crucified, died, and was buried;
>> he descended into hell.
>> The third day he rose again from the dead.
>> He ascended into heaven
>> and is seated at the right hand of God
>> the Father Almighty.
>> From there he will come to judge the living and the dead.
>
> I believe in the Holy Spirit,
>> the holy catholic church,
>> the communion of saints,
>> the forgiveness of sins,
>> the resurrection of the body,
>> and the life everlasting. Amen.[10]

THE NICENE CREED (AD 325; PRESENT FORM AD 589)

The Nicene Creed is a statement of the orthodox faith of the early Christian church in opposition to certain heresies, especially Arianism. These heresies, which disturbed the church during the fourth century, concerned the doctrine of the trinity and of the person of Christ. Because its unique phrases are meant more to defend than explain the faith, the Nicene Creed has always been used more for teaching than for worship.[11]

> We believe in one God, the Father Almighty,
>> Maker of heaven and earth,
>> of all things visible and invisible.
>
> And in one Lord Jesus Christ, the only-begotten Son of God,
>> begotten of his Father before all worlds,
>> God of God, Light of Light, very God of very God,
>> begotten, not made, being of one substance with the Father;
>> by whom all things were made;
>> who for our salvation came down from heaven,
>> and was incarnate by the Holy Spirit of the virgin Mary,
>> and was made man;
>> and was crucified also for us under Pontius Pilate;
>> he suffered and was buried;
>> and the third day he rose again according to the Scriptures,
>> and ascended into heaven,
>> and is seated at the right hand of the Father,
>> and he shall come again, with glory, to judge both
>> the living and the dead,
>> whose kingdom shall have no end.
>
> And we believe in the Holy Spirit, the Lord and giver of life,
>> who proceeds from the Father and the Son;
>> who with the Father and the Son together
>> is worshipped and glorified;
>> who spoke by the prophets;
>> and we believe in one holy catholic and apostolic church;
>> we acknowledge one baptism for the remission of sins;
>> and we look for the resurrection of the dead,
>> and the life of the world to come. Amen.[12]

Confessions

The Belgic Confession (1561)

The Belgic Confession's chief author was Guido de Brés (1522–1567), a Reformed itinerant pastor. During the sixteenth century, the Reformed churches in the Netherlands experienced severe persecution at the hands of Philip II of Spain, an ally of the Roman Catholic Church. In 1561, de Brés prepared this confession in French as an apology for the persecuted band of Reformed believers in the Lowlands. De Brés was most likely assisted by fellow pastors who wanted to prove to their persecutors that the adherents of the Reformed faith were not rebels, but law-abiding citizens who professed biblical doctrines.[13]

The Belgic Confession basically follows what has become the traditional doctrinal order of Reformed systematic theology: the doctrines concerning God (theology proper, articles 1–11), man (anthropology, articles 12–15), Christ (Christology, articles 16–21), salvation (soteriology, articles 22–26), the church (ecclesiology, articles 27–35), and the last things (eschatology, article 37). Article 36 addresses the theocratic nature of civil government.

Though it follows an objective doctrinal order, this confession has a warm, experiential, and personal spirit—facilitated, in part, by its repeated us of the pronoun *we*.[14]

Article 2: The Means by Which We Know God:

We know him by two means: First, by the creation, preservation, and government of the universe, since that universe is before our eyes like a beautiful book in which all creatures, great and small, are as letters to make us ponder the invisible things of God: his eternal power and his divinity, as the apostle Paul says in Romans 1:20. All these things are enough to convict men and to leave them without excuse. Second, he makes himself known to us more openly by his holy and divine Word, as much as we need in this life, for his glory and for the salvation of his own.[15]

Article 11: The Deity of the Holy Spirit:

We believe and confess also that the Holy Spirit proceeds eternally from the Father and the Son—neither made, nor created, nor begotten, but only proceeding from the two of them. In regard to order, he is the third person of the Trinity—of one and the same essence, and majesty, and glory, with the Father and the Son. He is true and eternal God, as the Holy Scriptures teach us.[16]

The Westminster Confession of Faith (1647)

The Westminster Confession of Faith has undoubtedly been one of the most influential documents of the post-Reformation period of the Christian Church. It is a carefully worded exposition of seventeenth-century Reformed theology after it had passed through the sharp conflict with Arminianism in Holland, and as it had shaped itself in the minds of

Scottish Presbyterians and English Puritans during their conflict with the leadership of the Anglican church.[17]

The various documents composed by the Assembly proceeded through a process of committee work in the afternoons, followed by plenary discussion on the floor of the Assembly in the mornings, with regular additional gatherings for worship and fast days. Despite disagreements, the divines produced one of the truly monumental documents of church history, which has "instructed, directed, and profoundly influenced Presbyterian churches worldwide ever since." The Confession of Faith, alongside the Shorter Catechism, has influenced Presbyterianism even more profoundly than Calvin's *Institutes*.[18]

Divided into thirty-three chapters, the Westminster Confession of Faith covers the whole range of Christian doctrine, beginning with Scripture as the source of knowledge of divine things. It continues with an exposition of God and his decrees, creation, providence, and the fall (II–VI) before turning to expound the covenant of grace, the work of Christ, and the application of redemption (X–XVIII).

While criticism is sometimes voiced that the confession is a deeply "scholastic" document (e.g., it has no separate chapter on the Holy Spirit), it is now increasingly noted that it is the first confession in the history of Christianity to have a separate chapter on adoption (XII)—perhaps the least scholastic of all doctrines.[19]

Beeke notes that "While the confession was composed by disciplined theological minds, it also displays the influence of men with deep pastoral and preaching experience. It is an outstanding expression of classical Reformed theology framed for the needs of the people of God."[20]

Chapter V, Article I: Of Providence

God, the great Creator of all things doth uphold, direct, dispose, and govern all creatures, actions, and things, from the greatest even to the least, by his most wise and holy providence, according to his infallible foreknowledge, and the free and immutable counsel of his own will, to the praise of the glory of his wisdom, power, justice, goodness, and mercy.[21]

Chapter VIII, Article I: Of Christ the Mediator

It pleased God, in his eternal purpose, to choose and ordain the Lord Jesus, his only begotten Son, to be the Mediator between God and man, the Prophet, Priest, and King, the Head and Savior of his church, the Heir of all things, and Judge of the world; unto whom he did from all eternity give a people, to be his seed, and to be by him in time redeemed, called, justified, sanctified, and glorified.[22]

Catechisms

THE HEIDELBERG CATECHISM (1563)

The Heidelberg Catechism originated in one of the few pockets of Calvinistic faith in the Lutheran and Catholic territories of Germany. Conceived originally as a teaching instrument to promote religious unity, the catechism soon became a guide for preaching as well. It is a remarkably warm-hearted and personalized confession of faith, "eminently deserving of its popularity among Reformed churches to the present day."[23]

The Heidelberg Catechism's 129 questions and answers are divided into three parts, patterned after the book of Romans. After an introduction about the true believer's comfort, questions 3–11 cover the experience of sin and misery (Rom. 1—3:20); questions 12–85 cover redemption in Christ and faith (Rom. 3:21—11:36), along with a lengthy exposition of the Apostles' Creed and the sacraments; questions 86–129 cover true gratitude for God's deliverance (Romans 12–16), primarily through a study of the Ten Commandments and the Lord's Prayer. The catechism presents doctrines with clarity and warmth. Its content is more subjective than objective, more spiritual than dogmatic. Not surprisingly, this personal, devotional catechism, as exemplified by its use of singular pronouns, has been called "the book of comfort" for Christians.[24]

> Question 1: What is your only comfort in life and in death?
>
> That I am not my own, but belong—body and soul, in life and in death—to my faithful Savior Jesus Christ. He has fully paid for all my sins with his precious blood, and has set me free from the tyranny of the devil. He also watches over me in such a way that not a hair can fall from my head without the will of my Father in heaven: in fact, all things must work together for my salvation. Because I belong to him, Christ, by his Holy Spirit assures me of eternal life and makes me wholeheartedly willing and ready from now on to live for him.[25]

Question 86: We have been delivered from our misery by God's grace alone through Christ and not because we have earned it: why then must we still do good?

To be sure, Christ has redeemed us by his blood, but we do good because Christ by his Holy Spirit is also renewing us to be like himself, so that in all our living we may show that we are thankful to God for all he has done for us, and so that he may be praised through us. And we do good so that we may be assured of our faith by its fruits, and so that by our godly living our neighbors may be won over to Christ.[26]

THE WESTMINSTER LARGER (1648) AND SHORTER CATECHISMS (1647)

The Westminster Assembly produced two catechisms. The Shorter Catechism contains 107 questions to which, generally speaking, single-sentence answers are formulated. The pattern followed is broadly that of the Confession of Faith, but the theological definitions given are compact and concise. The Larger Catechism shares the theology and many of the characteristics of the shorter version, but covers more ground in greater detail. It contains 196 questions and answers. Through both of these catechisms the divines set out to provide a well-structured guide to applying the word of God in the practical context of everyday life.[27] The following are examples from the Shorter Catechism.

Question 1: What is the chief end of man?

Man's chief end is to glorify God, and to enjoy him forever.[28]

Question 34: What is adoption?

Adoption is an act of God's free grace, whereby we are received into the number, and have a right to all the privileges, of the sons of God.[29]

We are part of a rich heritage, passed down to us by many who literally lost their lives to articulate their faith. Words matter. As we use these creeds, confessions, and catechisms in our corporate worship settings, may we not profess our faith flippantly, but with a sober and grateful sense of the history and heritage of truth.

NOTES

1. Joel R. Beeke and Sinclair Ferguson, ed., *Reformed Confessions Harmonized* (Grand Rapids: Baker, 1999) ix.
2. *The Worship Sourcebook* (Grand Rapids: CRC, 2004) 150.
3. John M. Frame, *Worship in Spirit and Truth* (Phillipsburg: Presbyterian and Reformed, 1996) 104–5.
4. Robert G. Rayburn, *O Come, Let Us Worship* (Grand Rapids: Baker, 1980) 219.
5. *Ecumenical Creeds and Reformed Confessions* (Grand Rapids: CRC, 1988) 5.
6. Ibid.
7. Ibid.
8. Ibid., 6.
9. Ibid.
10. Ibid., 7.
11. Ibid.
12. Ibid., 8.
13. Beeke, *Reformed Confessions*, ix.
14. Ibid.
15. *Ecumencial Creeds*, 79.
16. Ibid., 88.
17. Philip Schaff. *The Creeds of Christendom* (Grand Rapids: Baker, 1990) 760.
18. Beeke, *Reformed Confessions*, xii.
19. Ibid.
20. Ibid.
21. *The Westminster Standards* (Suwanee, Ga.: Great Commission, 2005) 8.
22. Ibid., 11.
23. *Ecumenical Creeds*, 6.
24. Beeke, *Reformed Confessions*, x.
25. *Ecumenical Creeds*, 13.
26. Ibid., 53.
27. Beeke, *Reformed Confessions*, xiii.
28. *Westminster Standards,* 71.
29. Ibid., 74.

PART 3

Developing Gospel-Centered Worship Communities

In the third part of this book we will view worship from the *situational perspective*, emphasizing cultural and contextual issues by focusing on developing gospel-centered worship communities. In Chapter Eight we will discuss the importance of developing a worship identity by exploring the role of personal relationships, liturgical models, and cultural context. We will also discuss how to maintain a certain identity, while still highlighting diversity within a worship ministry. In Chapter Nine we will conclude by pulling many concepts together, exploring how to craft gospel-centered worship.

8

Developing a Worship Identity

G OSPEL-CENTERED WORSHIP communities are not created in a vacu-um. We have already discussed the roles of leadership and theology. In this chapter we will explore the nature of personal relationships, liturgi-cal models, and cultural context—issues related to developing the worship identity of a local church.

Investing in Personal Relationships

Casting a Vision for Gospel Community

A worship identity that is rooted in the gospel must be developed from a clear vision, starting with one's governing body, filtering down through one's staff, and out to one's congregation. The vision of our church is "to see the people of Atlanta captivated and compelled by Christ thereby trans-forming the city through the gospel." We believe at a deep level that the gospel changes everything. This belief is held by our session, is experienced within our staff, and is regularly communicated to our congregation in both the corporate context of worship and the more intimate context of small groups.

Casting a clear and common vision for gospel community is a vi-tal ingredient for developing gospel-centered worship communities. Unfortunately, it is possible for a given church to preach the centrality of the gospel to one's congregation and in one's small group ministry, yet op-erate from a more corporate paradigm at the staff level. This dynamic has the strong potential to create spiritual isolation amongst staff members, and thus, not allow the full dynamics of openness and transparency to be shared at a professional level.

My pastor wears many different hats as he relates to us as staff. At times he will approach me as my *boss*; at other times, as my *pastor*; still, at other times as my *friend*, sharing with me and other staff members his own personal struggles and trials. This is such a gift. When the senior pastor models vulnerability, a church staff is free to be very open and honest with themselves and with others.

The gospel should permeate every aspect of a church. This dynamic, however, must begin with the pastor and governing body of the church. If this kind of vision for gospel community is not held by the pastor and governing leaders, other staff members will only be frustrated if they are seeking these kind of relational dynamics. I would strongly encourage anyone who is applying for a worship position to first inquire about the church's vision for gospel community. Does the gospel truly permeate and influence all facets of the church, or is there a dichotomy between the way the staff relates and the way the members are encouraged to relate? This is the crucial context for developing gospel-centered worship communities. The next step is to communicate a clear philosophy of ministry.

Crafting a Clear Philosophy of Ministry

In my first year of seminary in Atlanta one of my course assignments was to develop a philosophy of ministry. Because I had just started a new worship leader position, the timing was perfect. However, the initial drafts of my assignment simply sounded boring. They didn't seem to capture the true vision of what I thought our worship ministry should be. Finally, I just let the vision flow in words that felt right to me. I crafted three statements that have served to guide what we do as a worship and arts ministry for five years:

Cultivating the Heart of the Psalmist

Recapturing the Story of Redemption

Celebrating the Gifts of Artistic Expression

These statements have been the mantra of our ministry and have served as beacons to help us navigate through change and evolve as a ministry. Most of the decisions we have made over the past five years have been an attempt to flesh out our vision, striving to attain the heart of those three statements by translating words into real-life ministry.

It is so important for leaders to really take the time to first *dream* about the vision for their church's worship ministry. This is the time for leaders to unleash their heart, creativity, and imagination—to really envision the kind of worship community they want to develop.

Then leaders have to take that dream and put it into *words*. This is the hard work of clearly articulating vision. Leaders should write clearly and allow their words to flow from who they are—trusting their instincts and recognizing that they have to really own this and believe it. Church leaders should not write vision statements that sound like someone else. They must be authentic to who they are.

Finally leaders must take those words and start putting them into *tangible forms of ministry*. This is where the real fun begins! Rest assured, things will never work out the way they were planned. A church's vision will be dependent upon the resources and personnel it has available. Leaders should be patient, taking small steps and doing things with excellence. Doing a few things well is better than trying to do too much that is only mediocre.

Developing Teams

PASTOR/WORSHIP LEADER

For a while, my pastor and I were the worship ministry team. We would meet in his office each week and put our heads together about the service. My pastor would share the text and theme, offering touch-points and anchors that helped me to think creatively as I began to craft each service. We have maintained this dynamic (though we may not always meet face-to-face), connecting each week on the theme and direction of the service.

WORSHIP MINISTRY TEAM

After being at East Cobb a couple of years I formed a *Worship Ministry Team*. This team met monthly to brainstorm direction for the ministry; discuss pertinent issues and initiatives that we would bring to our session; and plan for special seasons throughout the Christian year. As our ministry grew and as my vision for a worship *and arts* ministry really began to grow, I created a second team, a *Creative Arts Team*.

CREATIVE ARTS TEAM

The Creative Arts Team is made up of the members of the Worship Ministry Team, plus leaders in the following areas of ministry: visual arts, aesthetics, music, technical arts, drama, and dance. This team is made up of ten people who meet once a month. Now the Worship Ministry Team offers general oversight of the ministry, and the Creative Arts Team provides the creativity for planning special events and services as well as integrating worship and various artistic expressions.

These various teams emerged as we continued to take tangible steps to carry out the vision that I shared earlier; namely, to cultivate the heart of the psalmist, recapture the story of redemption, and celebrate the gifts of artistic expression. I knew at a deep level that I wanted to celebrate the gifts of artistic expression in our body, but I wasn't exactly sure what that would look like. I knew I wanted to develop an integrated worship and arts ministry, but I wasn't sure exactly what that would look like either. Vision has to be fleshed out. It is very much like a seed that is planted—it takes time for that seed to grow.

Ministry is about people, and it takes *people* to grow a ministry. Often, God will bring the right people with both the heart and passion for carrying out various aspects of a church's vision. I knew that creating a multifaceted worship and arts ministry would celebrate people's creative gifts and would give them an opportunity to serve and edify the body through their primary area of gifting.

Choosing a Liturgical Model

Part of fleshing out vision and developing a worship identity involves choosing a particular liturgical model. What style of worship will characterize a given church? There are many different liturgical models for a worship service. In this section I will outline several of these models, highlighting the distinct characteristics and contributions of each.

The Lectionary Model

The first model that we will explore is the Lectionary model of worship. This approach is highly liturgical and typically follows the Lectionary for Sundays, beginning with the First Sunday of Advent and following through the Christian year. This is the most structured and "fixed form" method of worship planning. The thrust of this approach is *to retell the story of redemption through word and sacrament both at the micro-level of the liturgy as well as at the macro-level of the Christian Year.*

Common Order of Worship (Lectionary):

- Gathering
- Greeting
- Hymn of Praise
- Opening Prayer
- First Lesson (Old Testament)
- Psalm

- Second Scripture Lesson (Epistle)
- Hymn
- Gospel
- Sermon
- Responses to the Word (Hymn, Creed)
- Prayers of the People (Pastoral Prayer)
- The Peace
- Offering
- Prayer of Thanksgiving
- The Lord's Prayer
- Hymn
- Communion
- Benediction

Of all of the models we will explore, the Lectionary model represents probably the oldest service style and format. This model would characterize most Anglican and Catholic services. Following the lectionary helps ensure a balanced service model as far as biblical texts—pulling each Sunday from the Old and New Testaments and the Psalter. However, this particular service has the potential to become a bit mechanical. Those leading these services must be careful to allow for some spontaneity and freedom within the rigid structure. They must also be somewhat sensitive to non-Christians, the un-churched, and new believers—those who would be unfamiliar with a lot of the liturgical rubrics—and should think of creative and pastoral ways of guiding them through the service so that it is meaningful to them.

The Traditional Model (Reformed or Revivalist)

Although less formal than the Lectionary model of worship, traditional worship still follows a planned and structured order. It would be accurate to describe this model as "semi-liturgical." The thrust of the Traditional model of worship is *to strike a balance between form and freedom, utilizing some liturgy and fixed forms, yet remaining skeptical of too much ritual, finding the highpoint of worship in the preaching of the word.* Because of historical developments, I will break the Traditional model into two distinct categories: Reformed and Revivalist.

TRADITIONAL/REFORMED

What we are describing as Traditional worship began to appear soon after the Middle Ages ended. It was a modification of medieval worship, intend-

135

ed to correct its abuses. Worship during the Protestant Reformation began to emerge into something different from the Roman Catholic Church. A modified liturgical style began to appear in Switzerland and England during the sixteenth and seventeenth centuries. These services, less structured than those fashioned by Luther and Cranmer, were the forerunners of our modern-day Traditional worship. John Calvin was the leading Reformer in Geneva, where he served as both pastor and city leader. He judged harshly the prevailing worship practices of the Roman Catholic Church. Under the long arm of Calvin and his successors, worship was changed into a less formal, more open style. Out of this evolution came a pattern of worship that is recognizable and powerful in today's church.[1]

Common Order of Worship (Traditional/Reformed):

- Prelude
- Silent Prayer
- Striking of the Hour
- Welcome and Announcements
- Call to Worship
- Hymn/Psalm
- Invocation and Lord's Prayer
- Creed
- *Gloria Patri*
- Pastoral Prayer
- Baptism
- Psalter
- Collection
- Prayer of Illumination
- Scripture Reading
- Sermon
- Response and Blessing
- Hymn/Psalm
- Benediction

Speaking to the tradition of Reformed worship Johnson writes:

> Given the whole history of Reformed worship, continental and British, ancient and modern, there has been a balance built around the liturgical use of the Ten Commandments, the Creed, the Lord's Prayer, and sometimes a written confession of sin. On the one hand, the Reformed tradition cautions us against over reliance upon liturgy. Such will lead to rote prayers [and] formalism . . . On the other

hand, a modest number of fixed forms can serve as a hedge against the deterioration of worship in eras of spiritual decline or when the gifts of the minister are not up to the occasion.[2]

TRADITIONAL/REVIVALIST

In America, the Traditional model of worship reflects its revivalist background in its love for gospel hymns. Hymn writers who figure prominently in the gospel hymns used in traditional worship include Philip Bliss, Fanny Crosby, B. B. McKinney, and Isaac Watts.[3]

Soloists and ensembles augment the choir in traditional services. The choir regularly sings traditional modern anthems, hymn arrangements by musicians like John Ness Beck, contemporary anthems such as those by Tom Fettke and Mark Hayes, and occasional contemporary popular music arrangements by Michael W. Smith and others. The organ and piano serve as the primary musical instruments in the traditional service.[4]

Common Order of Worship (Traditional/Revivalist):

- Piano Prelude
- Hymn
- Hymn
- Prayer
- Welcome and Announcements
- Solo
- Testimony
- Hymn
- Offertory Prayer
- Offertory
- Special Music
- Sermon
- Invitation Hymn
- Closing Chorus

In his book, *The Worship Maze*, Paul Basden offers the following comment on the Traditional model of worship:

> Traditional worship offers believers a warm yet structured way to offer praise to God. Seeking to include enough reverence to avoid tackiness and enough formality to avoid staleness, this style continues to appeal to many Christians. At its best, its provides a *via media* for those who do not like either liturgical worship or more

contemporary worship. At its worst, it simply provides a temporarily safe harbor for those who refuse to face the radical changes that have occurred in our culture over the last half-century.[5]

Having discussed the two primary models of Traditional worship, we will now explore two more recent models of worship: the Seeker model and the Praise and Worship model.

The Seeker Model

The Seeker model of worship developed largely in reaction to both the Lectionary and Traditional models of worship. I've heard testimonies of those from the Baby Boomer generation who had a very negative church experience growing up. Many would say that church was "irrelevant" and that it did not connect well with the rest of life. The Seeker model, developed largely by Willow Creek Church in Chicago, was the answer to this Baby Boomer generation crisis.

Though not as fixed as the Lectionary or Traditional models of worship in terms of Scripture readings and prayer, this model does follow a definite order and structure. The thrust behind this model is *to reach the unchurched and the de-churched through a relevant and topical message complemented by the creative and innovative use of technology and the arts.*

Common Order of Worship (Seeker):

- Music
- Drama
- Music
- Message
- Music/Dance

The goal of the Seeker model is to make church relevant for those who are either non-churched or who were bored with or disillusioned by the church growing up. In the Seeker model, the highly liturgical signs and symbols of the lectionary model have been replaced with drama, contemporary music, and messages geared toward peoples' felt needs. These services have proven to be very fruitful in breathing new life into worship and in reaching out and connecting in powerful ways to nonbelievers and to those who might have been brought up with a negative view of the church.

The Praise and Worship Model

A fourth approach is the Praise & Worship model of worship. This model thrives on intimacy, spontaneity and flow. The general pattern for this model is taken from the biblical call to "enter his gates with thanksgiving, and his courts with praise!" (Psalm 100:4). The thrust of this model is *to have an intimate, affective, Spirit-filled encounter with God through music and a message, culminating in a time of ministry, often involving the laying on of hands and prayer.*

Common Order of Worship (Praise and Worship):

• Songs of Invitation
• Songs of Thanksgiving & Praise
• Songs of Intimacy & Confession
• Message
• Songs of Consecration

Two major contributions that this service model has brought to the church are an explosion in contemporary worship music as well as a strong desire for God's Spirit and presence in corporate worship. People like Andy Park and Brian Doerksen (of the Vineyard movement) represent some of the highly influential worship leader/songwriters of the past two decades.

Though more could be said about the above service models, I will spend the remainder of this section discussing the Convergence model of worship. Many good books and liturgical resources have already been written on the above service models, and I would encourage further reading on these traditions.[6]

The Convergence Model

God has used each of the above models of worship in powerful ways to edify the church. In our present day and age, it seems that a convergence of the above models is taking place, hence, the name of our fifth and final model. The Convergence model seeks *to bring out the best of these various models of worship by creating a robust gospel-dialogue, a multi-sensory sacramental experience, and an affective, Spirit-filled encounter—each complemented by a creative and innovative use of technology and the arts.*

Robert Webber is a strong voice regarding this model of worship. His books *Blended Worship, Planning Blended Worship, Ancient-Future Faith* and *The Younger Evangelicals* unpack some of the history behind the emergence of this service style, such as the rise of postmodernism as well as a desire for authenticity and a more robust consciousness of heritage and tradition. Though this model is highly resonant with Webber's articulation of *blended* worship, I am intentionally using the word "convergence" because, for some, the term "blended" is focused more narrowly on just the *music* within a worship service (i.e., a *blend* of traditional and contemporary styles of worship music). The Convergence model (and Webber's Fourfold model) goes beyond just the musical considerations of worship.[7]

Common Order of Worship (Convergence):

- Prelude
- Gathering Hymn
- Call to Worship
- Hymns of Response
- Prayer of Confession
- Assurance of Pardon
- Hymn of Response
- Personal Testimony
- Offering
- Public Reading of Scripture
- Sermon
- Confession of Faith
- Hymn of Response
- Communion
- Benediction
- Postlude

This approach employs some of the structure, liturgical framework, and sacramental practice of the Lectionary model, but with more freedom. This model also seeks to celebrate the richness of the Christian year. Its desire to be word and gospel-oriented is influenced by the Reformed heritage of the Traditional model; however, it recognizes that the other elements of worship aren't merely a "warm-up" to the preaching of the word. The influence of the Praise and Worship model is evident by the desire for the liturgy to be truly Spirit-filled—not a mechanical exercise. Finally, the influence of the Seeker model is evident in the desire to unleash creativity and innovation by incorporating artistic expressions such as drama, dance, and multi-media technology.

This seems to be where the wind of God is blowing in worship communities today. Many congregations truly desire to embrace the very best of the old and the very best of the new. All of the signs and symbols of the

Christian faith are being re-introduced into the service of worship; yet, with a fresh sense of spiritual fervor, gospel-centrality, and gospel-driven innovation and artistry.

The Anglican Church in Africa, for example, has developed a new book of common worship entitled *Our Modern Services*. This worship resource indicates a strong desire for liturgy, but liturgy with Spirit-empowered life and creativity.

> It must be remembered that it is not necessarily a new prayerbook that will make worship lively; more so, it is the creativity of those who will be using it in leading the worship or conducting the various services. Our clergy and lay leaders must learn to be creative and innovative and make our worship time as enriching as possible . . . It is suggested that the worshipper does not use this book rigidly but rather the Spirit of God must be allowed to permeate every word and every line of every service.[8]

One church's dream articulates the dynamics we have been discussing regarding current trends and a Convergence model that incorporates word, sacrament, and Spirit:

> Throughout history there appear to be three primary streams of expression within the Church. One has focused on the Word of God, another the Spirit of God, and the other the sacraments. The tendency of church bodies through the ages has been to build on one of these to the exclusion and, at times, suspicion of the others. Some churches would be strong in the proclamation of the Word while neglecting the sacraments. Others would celebrate the Spirit and His gifts while neglecting the proper teaching of the Word. And others would faithfully offer the sacraments while neglecting to train their members in the necessity for every believer to study the Bible. But at certain times and in certain places their have been church families that have sought what we have come to see as the deepest place in God's heart. They have endeavored to see all three streams present and merged into one mighty river. It is a Church such as this that we dream of becoming.[9]

We will discuss the Convergence model in more detail in the next chapter, but I would encourage church leaders and those involved in casting vision for worship to prayerfully consider the above models.

Knowing One's Cultural Context

A second important consideration in developing a worship identity is knowing one's cultural context, inside and out. The cultures of mid-central Florida, suburban Atlanta, and urban California are vastly different. One church planter, when recently asked what his worship style was going to be, responded wisely by saying, "I don't know yet. I need to better understand our culture first."

This is a great way to think about worship identity. Just because a certain liturgical model works well in the inner city, doesn't mean it will translate in a suburban setting. A worship identity should grow, to some degree, out of the very culture in which a church exists. This is knowing one's cultural context from the "outside." One must be a student of the demographics and social character of a given community.

We have a missionary family that was sent from our church to minister in Belize. For two summers we have sent mission teams and interns to serve in various ways, investing time and energy in this kingdom endeavor. I have had the privilege of meeting and talking with one of the church planters in Belize and his family. As we talked about worship I was surprised to find out that the music they sing is mostly American/European in style. I assumed that they were singing in a more indigenous, Caribbean style, musically, but they are not.

Because the precedent for traditional hymnody has been established for so long, many now feel that to play worship music in an indigenous style would be wrong! This is an unfortunate example of not understanding the cultural and contextual perspective of developing a worship identity.

Thankfully, the Bible does not prescribe a certain style of music that is sacred. Though there are certain principles that are regulative, there are many circumstances that the Lord simply leaves to our discretion. Musical style and genre is one area in which there is much liberty and freedom of expression.

Another part of knowing one's culture and context is being able to discern the false gospels that characterize one's target ministry area. Our church recently crafted a Strategic Plan, a sixty-page document that lays out the vision and mission of our church over the next five years of ministry. In a section entitled, "Our Neighbors: A People Profile," two major false gospels were identified in our suburban-Atlanta community, The Suburban Professional Gospel and the Suburban Hedonist Gospel:

> Every culture, every city, and every person has been impacted by
> sin and is crooked. And every culture, city, and person has a set

of heart idols that they serve. They also believe and live by a false gospel, in order to save themselves from the damage that sin has brought into their worlds. The people in our community of Atlanta live by two false gospels: the Suburban Professional Gospel and the Suburban Hedonistic Gospel . . . Our gospel-centered strategy is focused on meeting the deepest needs of people, giving them opportunities to experience transcendence through worship, meeting their hunger for relationship with in small groups, and pointing them to an alternative purpose for their lives in giving themselves away in ministry.[10]

Knowing one's cultural context—its people and their own unique false gospels—is crucial for the life and ministry of a church, particularly as it develops its worship identity.

In writing this particular section I wanted to get the insights from someone who is on the front lines of understanding cultural context as it relates to church planting and developing a worship identity. I asked Bart Garrett, a good friend and Lead Pastor of Christ Church of Berkeley, to share some of his thoughts.

What I think we take for granted most as Christians in a post-Christian context is how foreign our language, ritual, and custom can be to those who do not embrace the historic, Christian faith as do we. To follow the public ministries of Paul and Jesus is to recognize that both had a keen awareness of their cultural milieu. They knew intimately the hopes, fears, and dreams of the people they were ministering to. They knew which cultural beliefs and practices were an impediment to the gospel (the idols of the culture), which beliefs and practices were ramps towards the gospel (those things which are true, beautiful, and good—as revealed through the common grace of God), and which beliefs and practices were distracting people away from the essentials of the gospel (potentially volatile issues such as slavery, the role of women, or marriage and the validation of divorce).

To learn the cultural context in which one ministers is to take the time to listen to her voice by asking a lot of questions of its people and its entities. It is a willingness to spend many hours in a coffee shop, in the pub, in the local bookstore, striving to grapple with the meta-narratives of that culture. What do people do with their free time? What music is in their iPod? How do they dress? How do they talk? How educated are they? What do they think about those who have the power? Do they feel empowered themselves? What are the symbols of the culture? What do they love about where they live? What do they not like about it? What are their concerns about Christianity? What about Christianity is attractive to them?

Additionally, please do not assume that you know your context by reading what Christian authors have to say about your context or about the people that live in your context. As worship leaders and pastors, one of our missions in a pluralistic society is to be able to articulate the objections to the Christian faith better than the objector can. We learn to do this by reading our local paper(s), by reading notable magazines, by listening to NPR, and by reading authors with objectionable belief systems.

In addition to knowing the cultural context from the "outside," one must also begin to discern the narrower cultural context "inside" the church walls. The reason for this is that a church should reflect something of the personality of its own people. I am a firm believer in celebrating the gifts within a local body, finding a place for the operatic vocalist and the harmonica player; the violinist and the electric guitar player.

Though it has been our church's paradigm to celebrate the gifts within the body, I need to at least note that some choose to pay professional musicians in their local context. I have several worship leader friends who pay professional musicians most Sundays because of the aesthetic expectations of their particular culture. Some of the benefits of such an approach include having a high standard of musical excellence and a reliable schedule of hired musicians each week.

Of course there are financial realities associated with paying professionals at market value. Some churches will simply not have the resources to pay professional musicians even if they have a desire to do so. More importantly, however, if creating gospel-centered worship communities is a value and a goal, hiring professionals who may or may not be connected with the life and community of the church and who may or may not be believers will definitely have ramifications. I would suspect that if a worship leader strives for gospel community among his or her musicians, one will have an uphill battle to climb if the musicians view Sunday morning simply as another "paying gig."

Each local community will have to wrestle with this issue. I would particularly encourage those involved in a church planting situation to consider the precedents that will be set (and subsequently hard to reverse) early in the life of the church as decisions are made in the area of worship and music.

Hiring a Worship Leader

A third consideration in developing the worship identity of a local church involves the hiring of a worship leader—whether it is a volunteer, part-time, or full-time capacity. Whoever is facilitating the worship of God—musically, liturgically, creatively—will have an influence on a church's worship identity. The instruments God uses to carry out ministry are flesh and blood people. We cannot escape the human factor associated with worship identity. This topic was discussed in depth in Part One.

Maintaining Identity, Highlighting Diversity

In this section we will discuss how to maintain a worship identity while still highlighting diversity. There are many reasons why this is an important philosophy to embrace. This philosophy can be particularly helpful for congregations that are seeking to bring out a different style or genre without creating two entirely different services (which can, unfortunately, lead to the undesirable result of creating two different congregations). Hopefully, congregations can be educated to realize that musical taste is not a reason to divide a body.

Reflecting and Celebrating the Diversity within the Body of Christ

One does not have to look very far to notice that the body of Christ is made up a diverse mix of folks. Throughout the history of the church we have, at times, invested our creative energy in Gregorian chant, Metrical psalmnody, Lutheran chorale, Reformed hymnody, Revivalistic hymnody, Plainsong, Pop, Gospel, Folk, Rock, Acoustic, Classical, Urban-Gospel, and Celtic. The list is as varied as cultures are diverse. In today's multicultural atmosphere, celebrating only one genre of music is a bit boring at best, prideful at worst.

At one moment in time any given song was "brand new." It is my prayer that people will realize the value of singing and writing new songs for worship, as well as celebrating the rich and diverse heritage we have at our disposal. What a shame it would be to waste such musical variety, culturally and historically.

One way for a local church to maintain a certain worship identity while still highlighting diversity is to intentionally and creatively offer a different "genre-orientation" from time to time. For example, our church's identity is built around a "blended" approach, musically (mostly utilizing a Worship Team that includes piano, acoustic and electric guitars, drums, bass, etc). However, on the third Sunday of each month, we highlight the folk and Celtic genre by utilizing our Acoustic Ensemble (acoustic guitars, Celtic drum, flute, violin, harmonica, mandolin). We also emphasize a more traditional genre of hymnody from time to time, utilizing an adult choir and orchestra (throughout Advent, Christmas, Holy Week, and Easter, and on months with a fifth Sunday). This type of approach allows a given congregation to experience and enjoy some of the richness of diversity without losing their main identity.

Drawing Out an Eclectic Mix of Musicians

Reflecting the diversity within the body of Christ will likely begin to draw out an eclectic mix of musicians. People will inquire about using their instrumental gift when they recognize that a church is open to diversity. A good rule of thumb to remember is that "musicians attract other musicians." When people start to see harmonicas and bagpipes utilized in worship, others will start coming out of the woodwork, but only once they feel that it is a fairly "safe" environment to do so. When musicians sense an air of exclusivity and/or pride surrounding a certain musical genre, they will be hesitant to come forward if their instrument doesn't "fit."

Creating Space for Instrumentation that Might Not Otherwise Fit

It is important to be intentional about creating space for various kind of instrumentation. This does not mean that a church should seek ways to include every last musician in its congregation. Aesthetic integrity and maturity are important values as well. However, if someone is of an appropriate skill and maturity level, it is important to expend the energy to find a place to celebrate that person's gift. This will encourage the individual and will edify the body.

When I formed our Acoustic Ensemble, I was able to utilize a mandolin, harmonica, celtic drum, and bagpipes. I would have had a more difficult time finding a place for these instruments on our Worship Team or Adult Choir. However, for the Acoustic Ensemble, which emphasizes a genre of music that utilizes these very instruments, I immediately found a place not only for the instruments—but ultimately and more importantly—for the people, themselves. I was able to say, "I have a place for you."

Building Community

I have had the privilege of witnessing our worship and arts ministry grow as we have branched out musically, offering various ensembles. I have witnessed a young high school musician encouraged by adult musicians; a graduate student excited by a sense of belonging through his instrument; and a bass player energized by getting his fingers loose again.

For me, this is when it really gets good—when you begin to sense "community" developing and not just a random mix of musicians showing up "to do their thing." Celebrating diversity, drawing out an eclectic mix of musicians—these are values that, ultimately, help build community and put people together from various ages, stages, and seasons of life. It truly begins to reflect something of the body of Christ, and it is a beautiful thing to see.

I try to spend some time at the end of my Thursday night rehearsals either discussing a topic related to worship, sharing personal prayer requests, or just hanging out. These are important dynamics to try to build into the fabric of one's worship ministry.

Keeping Things Fresh

Finally, highlighting diversity within a worship ministry will help keep things fresh. I know it's time to mix things up when I sense things feel too predictable. Changing up musical genres is one way to keep things fresh for your worship ministry. Stagnancy is not a healthy place.

Navigating Through Change

I want to close this chapter with a set of diagnostic questions. As human beings, we are always somewhat resistant to change. When it comes to implementing change in worship, passions and convictions can often cloud our thinking. Therefore, it is vitally important for those who have been given oversight of the worship ministry of a church to ask themselves the following questions any time change is discussed or implemented:

Is my resistance to this change a matter of:

(1) Principle?
Are we violating a biblical norm?

(2) Prudence?
Is this the right time to implement this change?

(3) Preference?
Is this a personal issue for me?

(4) Pride?
Is this a gospel issue for me?

Having strong convictions about worship matters is essential for those in leadership positions. However, at times we can mask our pride and fears with arguments that *sound like* spiritual and/or theological convictions. This is so detrimental to the peace and purity of the church. When it comes to discussing and implementing changes in worship practice, I hope that we can be mature and gospel-centered enough to admit our fears and strive for unity and peace within the body. Taking the time to honestly answer the above questions in a gospel-centered context can be a very fruitful endeavor. It may uncover certain idols we did not even know existed in our own hearts.

NOTES

1. Paul Basden, *The Worship Maze* (Downers Grove: InterVarsity, 1999) 56–57.
2. Terry Johnson, *Leading in Worship* (Oak Ridge: The Covenant Foundation, 1996) 7–8.
3. Basden, *The Worship Maze*, 60.
4. Ibid., 60–61.
5. Ibid., 65.
6. For more on the Seeker model of worship read: Nancy Beach, *An Hour On Sunday* (Grand Rapids: Zondervan, 2004); for more about the Praise and Worship model read: Andy Park, *To Know You More* (Downers Grove, Ill.: InterVarsity, 2002); for more about the Lectionary model read: Hoyt L. Hickman, Don E. Saliers, Laurence Hull Stookey, James F. White, *The New Handbook of the Christian Year* (Nashville: Abingdon, 1992) and *The Book of Common Prayer* (New York: Oxford Press, 1990).
7. Webber's Fourfold structure of worship includes: Gathering, Word, Table, Dismissal. Though Webber highly recommends and endorses this model, he did not create it. This is an historic, biblical model for the contour and dynamics of corporate worship. His books *Blended Worship* (Hendricksen, 1994) and *Planning Blended Worship* (Abingdon, 1998) provide much helpful and relevant information on this model of worship.
8. Anglican Church of Kenya, *Our Modern Services*, (Nairobi: Uzima, 2003) vii, ix.
9. The Church of the Apostles, "Our Dream for This Church," http://www.apostles-raleigh.org/about.
10. East Cobb Presbyterian Church, *Strategic Plan for 2005–2009*, 25–27.

Crafting Gospel-Centered Worship

THE WEEK-IN-WEEK-OUT rhythm of corporate worship makes it a highly formative factor in our lives in many ways—spiritually, socially, psychologically, intellectually, and emotionally. Because it is so regular, it is easy to underestimate its influence; however, the words, images, and expressions of worship are powerful, though subtle, influences in our lives.

So often we live life in a dislocated manner. We can so easily begin to live selfishly and independently, or we can get so easily discouraged by the harsh realities of life. Corporate worship—through the power of word, sacrament, song, prayer, and profession—paints another reality for us and places us in the context of a story larger than ourselves. Worship opens our eyes to the beauty of the gospel and *relocates* us in the eternal nature of God and his kingdom, in the context of community and relationship. It is for these various reasons that those planning worship should treat their task with the utmost level of care and intention.

Six Guiding Principles for Planning Worship

Before moving into the details, I want to offer six guiding principles for planning worship.

Start with the Word

A worship planner must let his creativity begin with the theme and message of the primary Scripture text. If worship planning begins to regularly start with newspaper headlines, cultural trends, and popular fads, our people are in trouble. People need to be fed on the word of God, not here-today-gone-tomorrow headlines. The word of God is much more interesting and intriguing than we give it credit. It is full of inspired stories and more than capable of fueling a lifetime of creativity and imagination.

Identify a Theme

Ideally, a theme will lend creative focus to a worship service without every element being tied to it. Elements within a worship service should not become wooden interpretations of a given theme; rather, they should be fleshed out intuitively.

For example, if a theme is "The Love of Christ," a worship planner should not feel like every song must have the word "love" in it. Think big picture. Let the theme be "teased out" rather than explained throughout the service. Here, the mind of the theologically informed artist/liturgist is invaluable—one who is comfortable working with intuition and instinct rather than with black and white, "spell-it-all-out" methodologies.

Find an Anchor

Once the overall theme has been selected from the word, a worship planner must find an anchor: a song, a creed, a prayer, a call to worship—something that will help him advance the theme and spark further creativity. This is more or less a way to get one's thoughts and ideas off and running. Teasing out an overall theme through some form of expression (song, prayer, etc.) helps build focused, creative momentum.

Choose Appropriate Texts

A worship planner should be intentional about choosing texts that reflect specific *elements* within a service and that follow the overall *contour* of the liturgy. For example, the choice of text for a communion invocation would be shaped, in part, by the nature of the Lord's Supper (the contour); however, it would also be shaped by the language that is characteristic of an invocation (the element).

Particular texts can also reflect and accentuate a key *theme*. For example (continuing with the idea of a communion invocation), if the overall theme for a worship service was "God's Faithfulness," a worship planner might intentionally employ certain sentences and phrases in this prayer that would emphasize that particular focus.

Look for Transcendent Moments

A worship planner must be aware of the affective combination of certain elements such as a prayer of confession followed by a hymn of response; a personal testimony followed by a special music; or the preaching of the word, followed by a prayer or by silence, leading into a communion hymn.

One should be sensitive to the somewhat intangible elements of space, silence, transition, and timing. These are the moments that can be planned to some degree, but that are ultimately up to the Holy Spirit to orchestrate and empower. This is where the innovators of the Seeker model of worship tend to shine. They are wise students of "transcendent moments." I am sure that some wrongly suppose that trying to create the opportunity for such moments is manipulative. However, God has created us with five senses and the ability to receive information in a variety of ways. We would be neglecting the way God created us as multi-sensory beings if we did not seek to orchestrate the mysterious combinations of things such as melody and text; dance and song; word and image. This principle is acknowledged in a classic hymn: "For the joy of ear and eye, for the heart and mind's delight, For the mystic harmony linking sense to sound and sight, Lord of all, to thee we raise, this our hymn of grateful praise."[1] A worship planner should be a wise student of the human heart and the various ways human beings receive information.

Handle with Care

Finally, a worship planner must remain intentional even in the midst of often frantic planning. A worship planner must realize that this is the "priestly" aspect of his ministry and that the various elements he is selecting have tremendous potential to open people's eyes to the beauty of the gospel and transform people's lives in radical ways. This final principle simply underscores the formative character of worship and its powerful potential to relocate worshippers through the media of story, imagery, and expression.

Putting It All Together (Convergence Model)

In describing the various liturgical models in the previous chapter, I will reiterate that books on the Lectionary, Traditional, Seeker, and Praise and Worship models of worship already exist. Thus, for the purposes of this book, I will discuss how to craft a worship service based on the Convergence model of worship. In this section I am seeking to bring together the theological ideas discussed in Part Two, addressing the four characteristics of the Convergence model: (1) a robust gospel-dialogue, (2) a multi-sensory sacramental experience, and (3) a Spirit-filled encounter—each complemented by (4) a creative and innovative use of technology and the arts.

151

A Robust Gospel-Dialogue

In discussing a gospel-dialogue we are talking about the dynamic of how God speaks to us and how we respond. In a broad sense, this dynamic takes place as God speaks to us through word and sacrament, and as we respond through song, prayer, and profession. For this discussion, however, I want to focus on the specific texts we use in worship (songs, prayers, scriptures, creeds) and offer some ways to weave together the words we use as a gospel-dialogue. I will also highlight various practical considerations as well.

Choose a Song to be Sung as a Prelude

This song can be sung by the worship team only and could follow a medley of songs played instrumentally. This can be a strategic way of doing two things at once: (1) introducing new songs and (2) preparing people for worship. This song can also be sung again as a postlude.

Choose an Appropriate Gathering Song

This first congregational song should reflect something of the horizontal dimension of worship and possibly the vertical dimension of worship. It could also be an exhortation to worship (e.g., "Come, Now is the Time to Worship," "Come, Christians, Join to Sing").

Choose a Call to Worship

This is a summons to worship that is usually taken directly from a scriptural passage or that is *based* on a scriptural passage. It can be read responsively or by one voice. The call to worship establishes the unique purpose of the worship service and reinforces the "vertical dimension" of worship—an encounter between God and the gathered congregation—usually by offering: a description of the character of God (i.e., Isaiah 6:1-3—God's holiness; Colossians 1:15-23—the supremacy of Christ); or an exhortation to worship (Psalm 95, Psalm 150, Colossians 3:16).

Choose Hymns and Psalms of Response

(Throughout this discussion I am employing my definition of "hymn" from Chapter Five, thus referring broadly to: traditional hymns, re-written hymns, modern hymns, and contemporary worship music). These could be songs that either directly reflect the message of the call to worship or that further reinforce the vertical dimension of worship. This is also a place where a psalm could be sung. As noted in Chapter Five, the regular singing of the Psalms is a powerful way to sing God's word back to him and to express various themes that are not typically captured in hymnody (lamentation, doubt, etc.).

Select a Prayer of Confession and Assurance of Pardon

This could either tie-in with the theme of the sermon or it could flow out of the selection of songs that came before it. The language of this prayer (whether printed or not) can be specific or general in nature. As noted in Chapter Six, this is a very poignant place to emphasize a robust gospel. In other words, an honest, blunt, and visceral prayer of confession followed by a strong, scriptural assurance of the pardoning grace of God is a powerful way to articulate the gospel within the liturgy. However, if the prayer of confession is consistently sugar-coated and tepid, people will subtly begin to believe that their sin really doesn't go that deep and, thus, God's forgiveness and grace really isn't all that amazing. I will often preface the time of confession by saying something like this:

> We believe deeply in the power of the gospel. We believe that it is a like a double-sided coin: on the one hand we are more sinful than we could ever dare imagine; but on the other hand, we are more loved and forgiven than we could ever dare hope! For this reason we can now come boldly and honestly, confessing our sins before God and then hearing his words of pardon and grace spoken over us.

Select a Musical Composition During the Offering

Like a prelude selection, this can be selected intentionally, either (1) to introduce a new song or (2) to capitalize on the theme of the sermon to follow.

Select the Primary Scripture Text for the Ministry of the Word

Hopefully this decision will have been made weeks or months in advance of a given worship service. My pastor tries to preach on a rotating cycle, focusing on (1) a Gospel, (2) a major New Testament letter, (3) an historical book, and (4) spirituality every four years. This isn't as fixed as preaching through the Lectionary; however, it ensures a healthy diet of Scripture.

During the summer, I am usually given a layout for the upcoming ministry year, including primary Scripture texts and titles for each sermon.

Select an Appropriate Creed, Confession, or Catechism

The recitation of creeds and confessions can be a poignant way to respond to the hearing of the word, carrying with it a strong sense of heritage. However, professing our faith (through creed, confession, or catechism) *before* the message is a way to highlight a theme that will be unpacked throughout the service. Some examples of creeds, confessions, and catechisms were offered in Chapter Seven.

Choose an Appropriate Closing Hymn

This is where aesthetic choices are key! Often, non-musical pastors make the mistake of choosing a hymn based solely on lyrics, with little or no consideration of melody. To have the desired response, a given hymn has to be sing-able. Some older hymns may be great, textually, but dated melodically and/or harmonically. When doubtful of a given song's accessibility, ask someone (if possible) who can read music. Alternatively, one could look through the index of meters (in a hymnal) and select a more familiar tune for a particular hymn text.

In concluding this particular section I want to bring attention to some places where Scripture texts are utilized: (1) call to worship, (2) assurance of pardon, (3) Psalms, (4) sermon text. These are key places where God is speaking to us in the gospel-dialogue. Extra-biblical words are often expressed in our: (1) songs and hymns, (2) prayers of confession, (3) professions of faith. This dynamic is intentional and underscores the importance of having both Scripture texts as well as crafted words in worship.

A Multi-Sensory Sacramental Experience

Another powerful way that the Lord speaks to us in a gospel-dialogue is through the sacraments. In Chapter Four we discussed both the theology of the Lord's Supper and baptism as well as some liturgical considerations surrounding the administration of these two sacraments. Here we will reflect on some of those liturgical considerations for the Lord's Supper as they relate to the flow and contour of a worship service. This is where we can learn from our Anglican brothers and sisters and their rich sacramental practice.

SELECT A COMMUNION HYMN

It would be very appropriate for this hymn to be Christo-centric in nature. Some examples I often use are: "Jesus, Thou Joy of Loving Hearts," "Nothing but the Blood of Jesus," and "The Wonderful Cross."

SELECT A COMMUNION INVOCATION

Communion prayers were discussed in Chapter Six. The invocation could be prayed extemporaneously or it could be written.

SELECT A EUCHARISTIC PRAYER

There is always room for form and freedom, thus this prayer could also be prayed extemporaneously or it could also be a more lengthy, written or studied prayer.

CHOOSE A METHOD OF DISTRIBUTING THE ELEMENTS

This is a very important decision. Again, trying to strike a balance between form and freedom, no one method must always be used. However, too much change regarding the way the elements of the Lord's Supper are distributed can quickly cause confusion, thus taking away from the experience of the sacrament. I feel strongly that the sacrament of the Lord's Supper should encourage participation on the part of believers, thus emphasizing the "communion" aspect of this sacrament. For this reason, having the people come forward to receive the elements is a very physical way of achieving a sense of participation. As noted in Chapter Four, this is also a very appropriate place to have the elders of the church pray for individuals and/or families. It is also important to decide whether or not people will drink from a common cup.

CHOOSE SONGS TO BE SUNG OR PLAYED INSTRUMENTALLY

Here, decisions can be made to either have the congregation participate by singing or by having only the worship team sing fostering an environment for prayer and reflection on the part of the people as they receive the elements. Of course, this could also be a time for just instrumental music or for silence (or both). Again, it is not necessary for any rigid order; however, it is important for those crafting worship to give careful and intentional thought as to why certain decisions and choices are made.

Incorporate Prayers for Those Not Communing

Some carefully crafted written prayers can provide a wonderful way for those not communing to still participate during this time of the worship service. Here are some examples:[2]

Prayer for Those Searching for Truth:

> Lord Jesus, you claim to be the way, the truth, and the life. Grant that I might be undaunted by the cost of following you as I consider the reasons for doing so. If what you claim is true, please guide me, teach me, and open to me the reality of who you are. Give me an understanding of you that is coherent, convincing, and that leads to the life that you promise. Amen.

Prayer of Belief:

> Lord Jesus, I admit that I am weaker and more sinful than I ever before believed, but through you I am more loved and accepted than I ever dared hope. I thank you for paying my debt, bearing my punishment on the cross, and offering forgiveness and new life. Knowing that you have been raised from the dead, I turn from my sins and receive you as Savior and Lord. Amen.

Prayer for Those Struggling with Sin:

> Lord Jesus, grant that I may see in you the fulfillment of all my need, and may turn from every false satisfaction to feed on you, the true and living bread. Enable me to lay aside the sin that clings so closely, and run with perseverance the race set before me, looking to you, the pioneer and perfecter of my faith. Amen.

Prayer of Commitment:

> Lord Jesus, you have called us to follow you in baptism and in a life of committed discipleship in your church. Grant that I may take the necessary steps to be one with your people, and live in the fullness of your Spirit. Amen.

SELECT A PRAYER AFTER COMMUNION

This is an appropriate place to incorporate some specific prayers of intercession for the body—remembering those who are ill, struggling, etc. As noted in Chapter Six, this prayer should also ring the note of thanksgiving.

An Affective, Spirit-Filled Encounter

I'll be honest; it's hard to talk about the dynamics of a Spirit-filled encounter without sounding somewhat mechanical. Nonetheless, there are some lessons we can learn from our charismatic brothers and sisters. In my particular heritage (Presbyterian) we are somewhat jokingly referred to as the "frozen chosen." We can learn a lot from those who feel uninhibited to express themselves physically and affectively in worship. Such freedom of expression brings an atmosphere of "expectancy" to the worship gathering.

INCORPORATING BIBLICAL GESTURES OF WORSHIP

In scripture we hear the call to "clap your hands," "shout," "lift up your hands," "bow," "dance." These are all very physical ways of expressing our affections before the Lord. In our Western culture, we are usually much more reserved in our corporate worship settings. However, God has created us body and soul, and thus, we must be careful not to neglect these biblical exhortations in Scripture.

SINGING SONGS TO GOD

In Chapter Five we discussed the dynamic of singing to and about God. Here, we can experience the powerful dynamic of singing songs directly to God—telling him (through the affective combination of text and tune) that we love him; that he is to be exalted; that he is our healer; that we stand in awe of him.

OFFERING SPONTANEOUS PRAYERS OF ADORATION AND THANKSGIVING

Incorporating spontaneous prayers in worship is a potent means of creating a "present" encounter with our heavenly Father. We should be as bold with our spontaneous prayers as we are with our written and studied prayers.

157

LIFTING OUR HANDS BEFORE THE LORD

This is a very liberating form of expression. Again, this is not meant to sound manipulative, such as "If you raise your hands you're more spiritual." However, the reason that people are not more expressive in corporate worship is often a matter of pride. We can be so fixed on ourselves in worship—worried about what others may think—that we become inhibited. It is my prayer that we become less and less *self*-conscious and more and more *God*-conscious in our corporate worship gatherings—that we would become "lost in wonder, love, and praise."[3]

Of course, an affective encounter with the Lord must be cultivated, not just in the corporate setting, but in the privacy of our homes as well. Feeling the intimacy of the Father in corporate worship assumes the private, one-on-one relationship with him throughout the rest of the week. Otherwise, our worship expressions *will* seem somewhat mechanical and contrived if we are not cultivating an intimate, affective relationship with him in our own personal times of worship.

A Creative and Innovative Use of Technology and the Arts

The church has long maintained a relationship with technology. Providentially, the advent of the printing press during the sixteenth century was a contributing factor in the widespread communication of the ideas of Luther and others that ultimately gave rise to the Reformation. Today, the founders of the Seeker model of worship have offered the church various means of using technology and the arts in powerful ways in worship. There is so much good technology now available for projecting things such as song lyrics, art, and video, that churches should seriously consider if and how they would like to incorporate such media. In Chapter Three I discussed the various ways that churches can respond to presentational technologies (reject, adopt, adapt, create). Here, I would simply offer some more liturgical considerations regarding the use of technology and the arts in light of crafting a worship service.

USING VIDEO OR PHOTOGRAPHS TO MAKE A SERMON ILLUSTRATION

Most projection systems are linked to both a computer and a DVD (and/or VHS) player. This offers the ability to play portions of movies as sermon illustrations (assuming that the appropriate licenses and procedures have been followed). Photographs can also be easily uploaded and used for visual effect.

USING A VIDEO SEGMENT TO SHARE A PERSONAL TESTIMONY

If this is done well it can be an effective means of sharing a personal testimony within the flow of a worship service. The use of editing and the ability to have multiple takes will help ensure that the message is communicated accurately and effectively, particularly for someone who gets nervous talking in front of people.

CREATING VIDEO SEGMENTS TO HIGHLIGHT VISION OR CAPTURE A THEME

The use of video technology can be an effective means to speak to people's eyes and imagination in ways that words simply cannot. Short films segments can be created to cast church vision or to capture a particular theme. These video segments can be strategically placed within a service so that the flow of worship is only enhanced, not interrupted.

INCORPORATING DRAMA TO COMPLEMENT THE PREACHING OF THE WORD

In Chapter Three we discussed the role of drama and how it can be used to (1) raise tension that the sermon resolves, (2) raise questions that the sermon answers, or (3) to offer a message from a first-person perspective. These are just some of the ways that drama can be utilized in the context of worship.

INCORPORATING DANCE TO COMPLEMENT THE MUSIC

I have heard it said that "dance is to the eyes as music is to the ears." Dance can be a very moving complement to the media of song. When done well, dance can bring a very worshipful expression to a sung musical offering. However, it can also stand on its own with only instrumental support.

Details that Make a Difference

KEY

Choosing appropriate keys for a congregation is very important. I've heard one worship leader say that his congregation sings from "C to shining C." Meaning that the range he tries to stay within covers an octave (starting at "middle C") on the piano. This is a pretty good rule of thumb to follow. However, it's nice to make the congregation "reach" for a given note from time to time—this adds to the passion and strength of a given lyric. If it's too high, most people simply won't go for it; they'll choose instead not to sing. Notes that are too low also take too much effort. Worship planners should strive to keep songs in moderate keys for the congregation. If necessary, simply transpose a given arrangement.

TEMPOS

Tempos are another important consideration. You don't want to have songs moving so quickly that the words get lost; however, you don't want to sing so slowly that it feels like a funeral! Balancing upbeat, moderate, and slow tempos is something the people will be aware of, intuitively. In other words, when a good balance is struck, people won't be thinking, "Wow, the worship leader really wove together a nice mix of songs with varying tempos." However, when executed poorly, they will think, "Wow, I'm about to fall asleep."

MODULATIONS

Like tempos, the congregation will feel key changes intuitively. They will sense when all of the last five songs "kind of sounded the same" (if they were all in the same key). And they will be aware of a stream of songs with no cohesion (when every song is in a different key with no smooth modulations). Thus, it is important not to sing every song in the same key, but to move from song to song, sometimes through modulations.

I am not a modulation fanatic. I do not believe that you have to have seamless music throughout an entire song set. I think it can be equally pleasing to have brief periods of silence—when a song ends and there is a short rest before a new song in a different key begins.

TRANSITIONS

Modulations are important because they are one means of bringing about transitions. Transitions are important for the overall flow and movement of a worship service. Too many rough transitions and the people get distracted. Smooth transitions can help facilitate people's engagement and focus within the context of corporate worship. Transitions at the *micro* level as well as the *macro* level must be thought through. Modulations are ways of transitioning between songs during the ministry of praise—this is at the micro level. Transitioning from the ministry of the word into the celebration of the Lord's Supper involves a change at the macro level. All of these transitions should be done with forethought, creativity, and pastoral sensitivities.

SPACE

At a basic level, worship simply involves "doing stuff." Worshippers are singing, praying, reading scripture, listening, taking sermon notes, etc. At some point, worship should involve simply "being." Carving out space in worship for people to simply "be" is an important consideration. I am not trying to imply that singing and other elements don't also involve this dynamic of being, but sometimes this dimension can simply get planned out of worship. People need time, in the context of corporate worship, to simply be still—this is actually a way of responding.

SILENCE

Silence is, of course, one way to try to carve out space in worship and allow the opportunity for people to be still. The irony of silence is that it can often become "distracting." We discussed this to some degree in Chapter Six when we talked about prayer. Often, when we are given a moment of silence, we don't know how to use it so we begin to fill it up *with ways of how to fill it up!* It is easy for our thoughts to wander randomly from one thing to the next.

I can't say that I'm an expert on this by any means, but a period of silence can be used well when it follows something with focus; for example, a Scripture text with particularly vivid imagery or a question or exhortation related to a sermon theme. Worship planners should give serious thought as to how to effectively carve out blocks of silent reflection in worship.

AESTHETICS

Making the most of the worship space is another important detail that can make a difference. We discussed the topic of aesthetics in Chapter Four. Are floral arrangements utilized? Are banners displayed in the sanctuary? Can you utilize works of art—paintings, photographs, and sculptures—in your worship space? The Aesthetics Team at our church makes all of the above decisions. This is more than just a "Flower Committee." These people have a gift for making space beautiful and thematic. This is an area all too often neglected in churches. Beauty should be embraced throughout the entire Christian year, not just during particular seasons; namely, Christmas and Easter.

PERSONNEL

Knowing who will serve a given worship service most effectively is an obvious but sometimes overlooked detail that can make a difference. We have around fifteen elders in our church; however, not all of them are equally gifted at speaking or praying publicly. There are a number of vocalists in the worship and arts ministry but not all of them are soloists. Knowing how to use people in the capacity that best suits them takes skill and discernment. Sometimes you simply have to learn through trial and error, but making personnel decisions is an important aspect of worship planning.

My pastor likes to jokingly remind me, "Sunday comes around every week!" Worship planners have both the awesome privilege and the daunting task of crafting gospel-centered worship each and every week. As we go about this task, I pray that God would unleash the creativity of his people and open our eyes to the beauty and paradox of the gospel through the art of worship.

NOTES

1. Folliott S. Pierpoint, "For the Beauty of the Earth," *Trinity Hymnal* (Suwanee, Ga.: Great Commission, 1990).
2. Church Bulletin, Redeemer Presbyterian Church, New York.
3. Charles Wesley, "Love Divine, All Loves Excelling," *Trinity Hymnal* (Suwanee, Ga.: Great Commission, 1990).

Epilogue

WHEN I came home for Thanksgiving break during my freshman year of college there were two annoying questions that everyone seemed to ask me: "What's your major?" which was followed by, "What are you going to do with it?" The "do with it" part annoyed me the most. What is implied in these three words is: "How are you going to make money?"

This way of thinking can be so discouraging for a young person with gifts and dreams and talents. A freshman in college is more than likely still figuring oneself out. Why limit one's calling and vocation to a path of moneymaking options?

In our American society, it seems that some pursuits are considered "real jobs," while others are not. The arts—music, theater, dance—are okay when one is younger, but not really considered "practical" pursuits as adults. Artist, Thomas Blackshear shares how "Somewhere along the way, people equated certain talents, especially the arts, with laziness or foolishness. But in truth, artistic and creative thinkers have helped shape our society."[1]

I love the movie *Dead Poets Society*. There is one particular scene in which Robin Williams—who plays the role of a very non-traditional literature teacher in a boys' preparatory school—huddles the boys up during a class on Romantic poetry. After humorously asking the boys to "rip out" the introduction to their textbook because of its uninspired treatment of poetry, he shares the following statement with much passion:

> We don't read and write poetry because it's cute. We read and write poetry because we are part of the human race . . . business, law, medicine, these are all noble pursuits needed to sustain life. But music, art, romance . . . these are the things we live for.[2]

I would add that we pursue the arts because we have been fashioned after our Creator who is passionate about beauty, art, and aesthetics. Therefore, "it is against our very natures to live predictable, unimaginative lives or to ignore creation's beauty."[3]

At a worship conference in Franklin, Tennessee, musician and author, Charlie Peacock, was asked the question, "How can the church begin to influence culture as opposed to culture always shaping the church?" I will never forget Charlie's response. He said, quite pointedly: "The church must recognize the legitimacy of a vocation in the arts."

This is such a profound statement. Can you imagine what might happen if the church began to recognize the need for art and creativity, really embrace it as a legitimate calling? At the very least, conversations about college majors around a Thanksgiving meal might reveal a different tenor. At best, we might begin to think more deeply about how we do ministry. We might begin to think more deeply about worship practice and, thus, provide better educational and instructive curriculums for an emerging generation of worship leaders. We might even begin to realize that for too long our Lord has found our desire for beauty, art, and creativity not too strong, but too weak!

I want to close this discussion on the art of worship with a challenge: Can we, as the Church, really begin to consider the legitimacy of a vocation in the arts? Can we begin to foster a vision for the arts in our local churches and communities? Can we gain a radical vision for cities and begin to influence the culture around us by cultivating a community of artists—not because art and creativity can occasionally be instructive or beneficial, but because we have been fashioned after our Creator God who is wildly creative and who loves beauty? As one worship leader has noted, "Artists need the church, but the church needs artists."[4]

Notes

1. Janice Elsheimer, Foreword in *The Creative Call* (Colorado Springs: Shaw, 2001).
2. *Dead Poets Society*, directed by Peter Weir (Touchstone Pictures in association with Silver Screen Partners IV, 1989).
3. Tom Jennings, "The Arts in Worship" (lecture notes on worship, Redeemer Presbyterian Church, New York, NY).
4. Ibid.

Appendix: Worship Resources and Websites

Musical Resources

1. Community Worship Resources (Christ Community Church): www.communityworship.com

2. Indelible Grace: www.igracemusic.com

3. Redeemer Music (Redeemer Presbyterian Church): www.redeemer.com

4. Christian Copyright: www.ccli.com

5. UK Worship (Kendrick, Townend): www.makewaymusic.com and www.kingsway.co.uk

6. Sovereign Grace Ministries: www.sovereigngraceministries.org

7. Lots of music resource materials: www.worshiptogether.com

8. Integrity Music: www.integritymusic.com

9. Maranatha Music: www.maranathamusic.com

10. Hillsong Music: www.hillsong.com

11. Song Discovery [best new worship music with lead sheets]: www.songdiscovery.com

12. Passion [Chris Tomlin, David Crowder, Charlie Hall]: www.sixstepsrecords.com

13. Vineyard Music: www.vineyardmusic.com

14. Psalms, Hymns, Spiritual Songs—Te Deum: www.tedeum.com/

15. Chorus Chords and Words: www.pwarchive.com, www.worshiparchive.com, www.worshipleaderassistant.com, www.praisecharts.com, http://freepraiseandworship.com

16. Hymn Words: www.cyberhymnal.org

17. Trinity Hymnal (original lyrics/traditional tunes): www.opc. org/books/TH/

18. Hymns Ancient and Modern (1861): www.oremus.org/ hymnal/am1861.html

19. *Gadsby's Hymns:* www.heritagebooks.org

20. Hymnals, instrumental arrangements, choral works: www.hopepublishing.com

21. Hymnals and Psalters: www.cgmusic.com/

22. RUF Hymnal Online: www.igracemusic.com/igracemusic/ hymnbook/hymns.html

23. Anglo-Genevan Psalter: www.canrc.org

24. D. A. Carson—Hymns and more: www.christwaymedia.com/

25. J. M. Boice—Hymns for a Modern Reformation: www.tenth. org/music/

Liturgical Resources

Prayer:

1. *The Worship Sourcebook.* Grand Rapids: CRC, 2004.

2. Old, Hughes Oliphant. *Leading in Prayer.* Grand Rapids: Eerdmans, 1995.

3. *The Book of Common Worship.* Louisville: Westminster John Knox, 1993.

4. *The Book of Common Prayer.* New York: Oxford University Press, 1990.

5. Engle, Paul E. *Baker's Worship Handbook.* Grand Rapids: Baker, 1998.

6. Bennett, Arthur, editor. *The Valley of Vision.* Carlisle, Pa.: The Banner of Truth Trust, 1975.

7. Johnson, Terry. *Leading in Worship.* Oak Ridge, Tenn.: Covenant Foundation, 1996.

8. *The Glenstal Book of Prayer.* Collegeville, Minn.: Liturgical, 2001.

Creeds and Confessions:

1. *Ecumenical Creeds and Reformed Confessions*. Grand Rapids: CRC, 1988.

2. Beeke, Joel R., and Sinclair B. Ferguson, editors. *Reformed Confessions Harmonized*. Grand Rapids: Baker, 1999.

3. *The Westminster Standards*. Suwanee, Ga.: Great Commission, 2005.

Software and Technology

1. Sibelius notation software: www.sibelius.com

2. Finale notation software: www.finalemusic.com

3. Multimedia systems: www.fowlerinc.com

4. Multimedia software: www.songshowplus.com, www.mediashout.com, www.highwayvideo.com, www.digitaljuice.com

General

1. Calvin Institute of Christian Worship: www.calvin.edu/worship/

2. Links to music, churches, articles, etc.: www.hotworship.com/

3. Guide to Christian Resources on the Internet: www.iclnet.org/

4. Barry Liesch worship resources: www.worshipinfo.com/

5. Arts and Worship, Paxson Jeancake: www.rhythmofworship.com

6. The Art of Worship: www.writeclik.com/worship_graphics

7. Worship Leader Magazine: www.worshipleader.com

8. Robert Webber's web page: www.ancientfutureworship.com

9. Special Music (Choral/Band/Orchestral) Resources: www.wordchoralclub.com

10. The Liturgy Fellowship: www.liturgyfellowship.org

---

*Many of these resources and websites were originally compiled for "The Sacrifice of Praise" worship conference hosted by Covenant Theological Seminary in St. Louis, Missouri (February, 2005).

Bibliography

Anderson, Herbert and Edward Foley. *Mighty Stories, Dangerous Rituals*. San Francisco: Jossey-Bass, 1998.

Anglican Church of Kenya. *Our Modern Services*. Nairobi: Uzima, 2003.

Augustine. *Confessions*. New York: Oxford University Press, 1991.

Baloche, Paul and Jimmy and Carol Owens. *God Songs*. Lindale: Leadworship.com, 2004.

Basden, Paul. *The Worship Maze*. Downers Grove, Ill.: InterVarsity, 1999.

Beach, Nancy. *An Hour On Sunday*. Grand Rapids: Zondervan, 2004.

Beeke, Joel R., and Sinclair B. Ferguson, editors. *Reformed Confessions Harmonized*. Grand Rapids: Baker, 1999.

Bennett, Arthur, ed. *The Valley of Vision*. Carlisle, Pa.: Banner of Truth Trust, 1975.

Berkhof, Louis. *Manual of Christian Doctrine*. Grand Rapids: Eerdmans, 1999.

———. *Systematic Theology*. Grand Rapids: Eerdmans, 1996.

Best, Harold M. *Unceasing Worship*. Downers Grove, Ill.: InterVarsity, 2003.

The Book of Common Prayer. Oxford: Oxford University Press, 1990.

Brown, Raymond. *The Message of Hebrews*. Downers Grove, Ill.: InterVarsity, 1982.

Burge, Gary. "Liturgical Worship." *Experience God in Worship*. Loveland: Group, 2000.

Calvin, John. *Commentary on Hosea*. Grand Rapids: Baker, 2003.

———. *The Institutes of the Christian Religion*. Louisville: Westminster John Knox, 1960.

Card, Michael. *Scribbling in the Sand*. Downers Grove, Ill.: InterVarsity, 2002.

Curtis, Brent, and John Eldredge. *The Sacred Romance*. Nashville: Thomas Nelson, 1997.

Davis, Sheila. *The Craft of Lyric Writing*. Cincinnati: Writer's Digest, 1985.

DeWaal Malefyt, Norma, and Howard Vanderwell. *Designing Worship Together*. Herndon, Va.: Alban Institute, 2005.

Doerksen, Brian. *You Shine*. Mobile, Ala.: Integrity Media, Inc., 2002 (compact disc).

Duck, Ruth C. *Finding Words for Worship*. Louisville: Westminster John Knox, 1995.

Dyrness, William A. *Visual Faith*. Grand Rapids: Baker Academic, 2001.

Ecumenical Creeds and Reformed Confessions. Grand Rapids: CRC, 1988.

Elsheimer, Janice. *The Creative Call*. Colorado Springs: Shaw, 2001.

Fee, Gordon D., and Douglas Stuart. *How to Read the Bible Book by Book*. Grand Rapids: Zondervan, 2002.

Frame, John M. "Music in Worship: Gateway to the Heart and Pathway to Controversy."

———. *Perspectives on the Word of God*. Eugene: Wipf and Stock, 1999.

———. *The Doctrine of the Knowledge of God*. Phillipsburg, N.J.: Presbyterian and Reformed, 1987.

———. *Worship in Spirit and Truth*. Phillipsburg, N.J.: Presbyterian and Reformed, 1996.

The Glenstal Book of Prayer. Collegeville, Minn.: Liturgical, 2001.

Grudem, Wayne. *Systematic* Theology. Grand Rapids: Zondervan, 1994.

Guinness, Os. *Fit Bodies Fat Minds*. Grand Rapids: Baker, 1994.

Hendriksen, William. *Exposition of the Gospel According to John, Volume II*. Grand Rapids: Baker, 1953.

———. *Exposition of the Gospel According to Luke*. Grand Rapids: Baker, 1978.

————. *The Epistle to the Ephesians*. Grand Rapids: Baker, 1967.

Hooker, Morna D. *Not Ashamed of the Gospel: New Testament Interpretations of the Death of Christ*. Paternoster, 1994.

Horton, Michael. *A Better Way*. Grand Rapids: Baker, 2002.

Hughes, Tim. *Here I am to Worship*. Ventura, Calif.: Regal, 2004.

Jeancake, Paxson and Allison. *The Rhythm of Worship*, 2003 (compact disc).

Jennings, Tom. "The Arts in Worship." Lecture notes on worship, Redeemer Presbyterian Church, New York, NY.

Johnson, Terry. *Leading in Worship*. Oak Ridge, Tenn.: Covenant Foundation, 1996.

Kavanaugh, Patrick. *Worship: A Way of Life*. Grand Rapids: Chosen, 2001.

Keller, Tim. "Glory." *It Was Good*. Baltimore: Square Halo, 2000.

Kidd, Reggie M. *With One Voice: Discovering Christ's Song in Our Worship*. Grand Rapids: Baker, 2006.

Kistemaker, Simon J. *Exposition of the Epistle to the Hebrews*. Grand Rapids: Baker, 1984.

————. *Exposition of the Second Epistle to the Corinthians*. Grand Rapids: Baker, 1997.

L'Engle, Madeleine. *Walking on Water*. Colorado Springs: Waterbrook, 1980.

Lewis, C. S. "The Weight of Glory." *The Weight of Glory and Other Essays*. Grand Rapids: Eerdmans, 1965.

Longman III, Tremper. *How to Read the Psalms*. Downers Grove, Ill.: InterVarsity, 1988.

————. *Reading the Bible with Heart and Mind*. Colorado Springs: NavPress, 1997.

Martin, Ralph P. *Worship in the Early Church*. Grand Rapids: Eerdmans, 1974.

McKim, Donald K. *Presbyterian Beliefs*. Louisville: Geneva, 2003.

Metzger, Bruce M. *The New Testament: Its Background, Growth, and Content*. Nashville: Abingdon, 1983.

Miller, Mark. *Experiential Storytelling*. Grand Rapids: Zondervan, 2003.

Milne, Bruce. *The Message of John*. Downers Grove, Ill.: InterVarsity, 1993.

Morgan, Robert J. *Then Sing My Soul*. Nashville: Thomas Nelson, 2003.

Morgenthaler, Sally. "An Open Letter to Songwriters." *Worship Leader* 13 (March/April 2004).

Moyers, Bill. *The Power of Myth*. New York: Anchor, 1988.

Mulholland, M. Robert. *Shaped by the Word*. Nashville: Upper Room, 1985.

Old, Hughes Oliphant. *Guides to the Reformed Tradition: Worship*. Atlanta: John Knox, 1984.

————. *Leading in Prayer*. Grand Rapids: Eerdmans, 1995.

Park, Andy. *To Know You More*. Downers Grove, Ill.: InterVarsity, 2002.

Pierpoint, Folliott S. "For the Beauty of the Earth," *Trinity Hymnal*. Suwanee, Ga.: Great Commission, 1990.

Pratt, Richard L. *He Gave Us Stories*. Phillipsburg, N.J.: Presbyterian and Reformed, 1987.

Sorge, Bob. *Exploring Worship*. Canandaigua, N.Y.: Oasis House, 1987.

Rayburn, Robert G. *O Come, Let Us Worship*. Grand Rapids: Baker, 1980.

Redman, Robb. *The Great Worship Awakening*. San Francisco: Jossey-Bass, 2002.

Roberts, Mark. *No Holds Barred*. Colorado Springs: Waterbrook, 2005.

Roff, Lawrence C. *Let Us Sing*. Norcross: Great Commission, 1991.

Rowland, Randy L. "The Focus and Function of Worship." *Worship Leader* 8 (May/June 1999).

Saliers, Don E. *Worship and Spirituality*. Akron, Ohio: OSL, 1996.

Schaff, Philip. *The Creeds of Christendom*. Grand Rapids: Baker, 1990.

Schultze, Quentin J. *High-Tech Worship?* Grand Rapids: Baker, 2004.

Siewert, Alison. *Drama Team Handbook*. Downers Grove, Ill.: InterVarsity, 2003.

Smith, Chuck, Jr. "A Taste of Heaven." *Worship Leader* 12 (January/February 2003) 22-25.

Smith, Scotty. *Objects of His Affection*. West Monroe, La.: Howard, 2001.

Stetzer, Ed. *Planting New Churches in a Postmodern Age*. Nashville: Broadman and Holman, 2003.

Stott, John R. W. *The Cross of Christ*. Downers Grove, Ill.: InterVarsity, 1986.

———. *The Message of Ephesians*. Downers Grove, Ill.: InterVarsity, 1979.

Tidball, Derek. *The Message of the Cross*. Downers Grove, Ill.: InterVarsity, 2001.

Townend, Stuart. "How Deep the Father's Love for Us." Kingsway's Thankyou Music, 1995.

Tripp, Paul David. *Instruments in the Redeemer's Hands*. Phillipsburg, N.J.: Presbyterian and Reformed, 2002.

Twit, Kevin. "What's in a Song? Turning Our Hearts," Reformed University Fellowship Website, http://www.ruf.org/sounds/whats1.htm.

VanGemeren, Willem. *Interpreting the Prophetic Word*. Grand Rapids: Zondervan, 1990.

———. *The Progress of Redemption*. Grand Rapids: Baker, 1988.

Webber, Robert E. *Blended Worship*. Peabody, Mass.: Hendrickson, 1994.

———. *Planning Blended Worship*. Nashville: Abingdon, 1998.

———. *Worship Old and New*. Grand Rapids: Zondervan, 1994.

Wesley, Charles. "Love Divine, All Loves Excelling," *Trinity Hymnal*. Suwanee, Ga.: Great Commission, 1990.

The Westminster Standards. Suwanee, Ga.: Great Commission, 2005.

White, James F., Hoyt L. Hickman, Don E. Saliers, and Laurence Hull Stookey. *The New Handbook of the Christian Year*. Nashville: Abingdon, 1992.

Willard, Dallas. *The Divine Conspiracy*. New York: HarpersCollins, 1998.

Wimber, John, Editor. "Songwriting" by Brian Doerksen. *Thoughts on Worship*. Anaheim, Calif.: Vineyard Music Group, 1996.

The Worship Sourcebook. Grand Rapids: CRC, 2004.